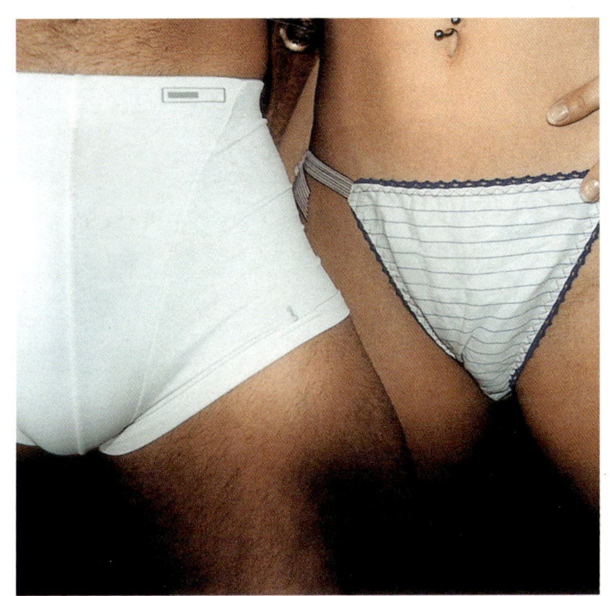

Erotic Home Video

Erotic Home Video
Create Your Own Adult Films

Anna Span

THIS IS A CARLTON BOOK

Text copyright © 2003 Anna Span
Design copyright © 2003 Carlton Books Limited

This edition published by
Carlton Books Limited 2003
20 Mortimer Street
London W1T 3JW

A CIP catalogue record for this book
is available from the British Library

ISBN paperback 1 84222 782 3
ISBN hardback 1 84222 947 8

Printed and bound in Italy

Editorial Manager: Judith More
Senior Art Editor: Barbara Zuñiga
Executive Editor: Zia Mattocks
Design: DW Design London
Editors: Lisa Dyer and Gordon Torbet
Production Manager: Janette Burgin

The author and publisher have made every effort to
ensure that all information is correct and up to date at
the time of publication. Neither the author nor the
publisher can accept responsibility for any accident,
injury or damage that results from using the ideas,
information or advice offered in this book.

Special photography © Anna Span/Television X, on the
following photographs: p.1, p.2, p.4 (right), p.5 (right),
p.8, p.9, p.10, p.13, p.35 (both), p.36, p.37, p.42, p.43,
p.44, p.48, p.49, p.59 (bottom), p.61 (both), p.67, p.77
(second from top, right, and third from top, both), p.78,
p.83, p.85, p.89, p.92, p.95, p.100 (both), p.101, p.102
(top), p.103 (top), p.107 (bottom), p.122, p.124.

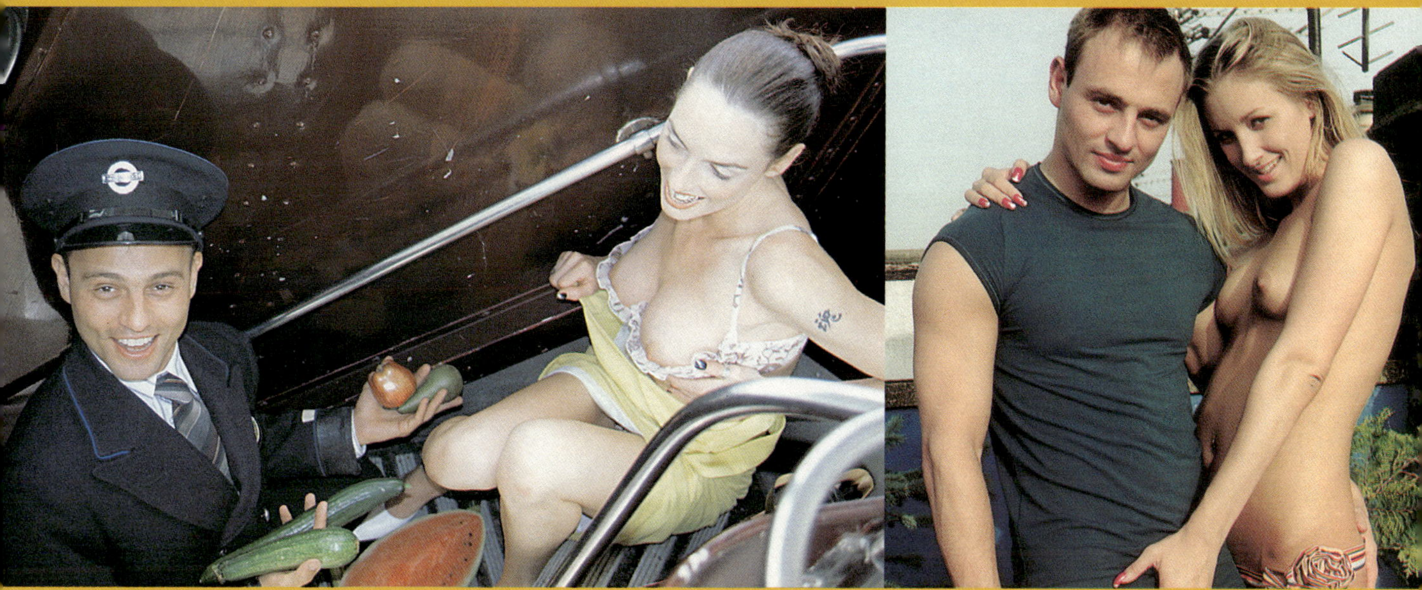

Contents

Introduction

Just think if you had the knowledge to make a video that satisfied completely your personal taste and your partner's. A film that didn't include all those shots that you have seen in commercial porn that you felt were a waste of time, or worse, were a turn-off. A film made in your own environment.

Have you ever fantasized about being a porn star?

Introduction

When I make commercial films, ultimately I have to cater to a wide audience of many differing tastes, but you can focus solely on what you like and nothing else. You can spend as long as you want making it; a truly personalized piece of entertainment that you can watch with your partner – again and again.

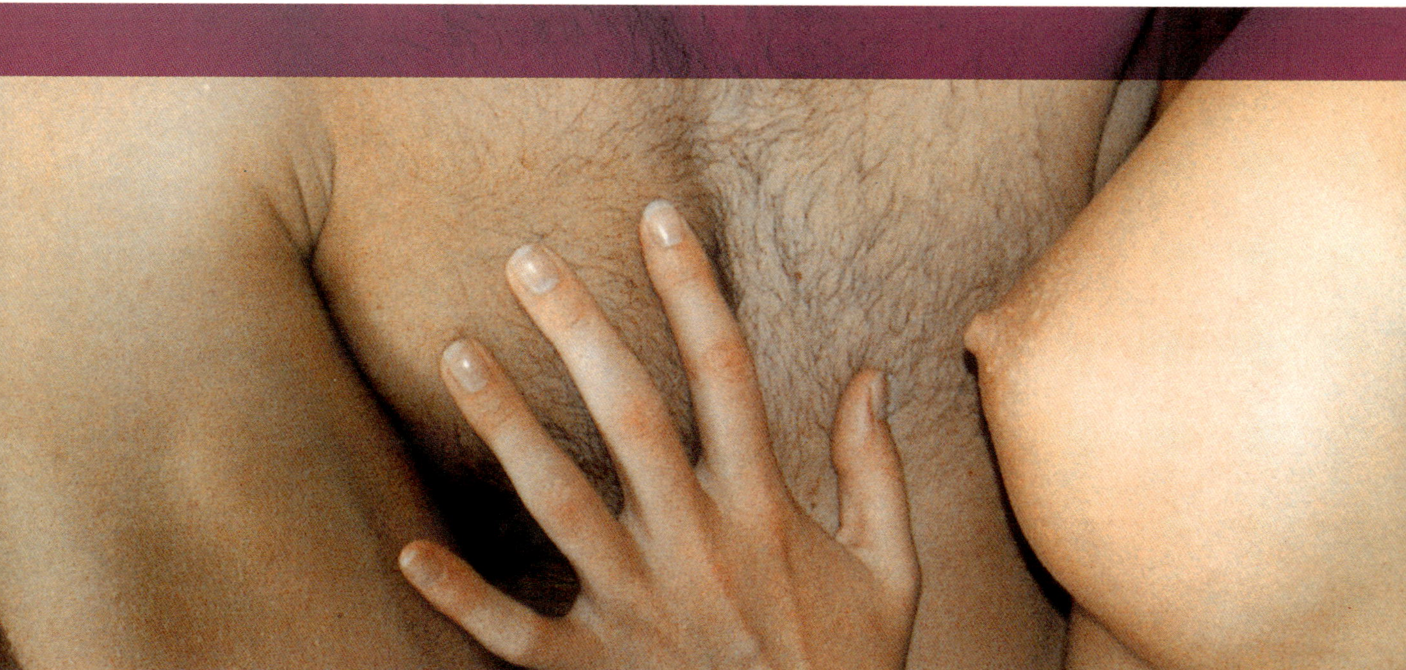

On a bookshelf containing so many other titles, what was it that made you pick up this particular book? What caught your eye? I know it was the word 'erotic', but what does that mean to you when placed with the word 'video'? What do these two words conjure up in your imagination?

Does it make you think of the way flesh looks under the glare of a video lens, of intimate sex exaggerated to the unreal? Does it remind you of glimpses of pornographic videos that you have seen, with their animal noises and lurid colours, their hard and bounding energy? A place of risk and power, maybe?

Or does it make you feel that sex is about intimacy? A shared place, an experience that the rest of the wide world doesn't come close to. Maybe you don't think about pornography – you are in love, and although involving a camera could be fun, it's not the same as porn. Is this a book that can help you on a journey towards greater intimacy for your partner and yourself? A book that encourages a safe place to experiment and to grow? Whatever your reasons for wanting to explore the art of erotic film-making, you're in the right place.

You can add all the personal touches you want in video.

WHAT WILL THIS BOOK TEACH YOU?

When you have finished reading this book – that is, if you're not away having sex – you will have learnt several things. There is a lot I can teach you about how to shoot an erotic film. There are the technical elements like lighting, using a camera and editing, as well as how to get the shots to make you both look like super porn stars,

But isn't pornography all about degrading women? And whether you are male or female, if you are interested in making a film, what sort of person does this make you? Are your fantasies normal? As a porn director, and especially as a woman, I find that people are very interested to hear about my experiences on the set during filming. What is it like to direct sex, to mix with porn stars all day, to watch people at it? These questions are inevitably followed up with the question 'So how do you go about getting into the industry, say as a performer?' I can say that around 80 percent of people I speak to harbour fantasies about being in a porn film, of being a sex symbol (or object), of being fantasized about, and being so attractive that the viewer is driven crazy with desire. A lot of people have fantasies about being filmed having sex, but are not so keen on actually forging a career out of it.

SOME THOUGHTS BEFORE YOU BEGIN

You want to make your own home-made 'blue' movie, but before you begin, have you really thought it through completely? Most people won't have any experience of being naked and having sex in front of a camera, so it is wise to give some thought to the questions that may crop up in the process. There are just a few things to consider before you shout 'Action!'

You need to go into this experience fully aware of the decision you have made and with the right protection (I'm talking legal, not contraceptive – but bear both in mind), so that you can relax and explore with confidence. You won't want to be half-hearted and holding back because you have unanswered concerns, only later to feel that you could have done better or been more confident in the final film. If this has been a secret fantasy of yours for a while, then take the time to make the most of it. Be honest with yourself and your partner now, with the view of engaging in a wholly enjoyable and positive experience.

Are you already in an established relationship in which you feel making an erotic film together could be a possibility? If you are reading this with the idea of going out to find a suitable partner for the experience

Natural performances are often the sexiest.

as well as what shots to avoid. There is advice on how to achieve the look you want, what locations to use (and which ones are illegal), as well as how to re-enact your fantasies as accurately as possible on the final film. And how to shoot your stomach so that it looks half its real size.

Perhaps more importantly, I have included sections on how to ask your partner about making a film together, how to discover fantasies that you didn't even know you had and communicate them. There are tips on performance, overcoming nerves, and how to feel good when you see yourself on video for the first time. I will also tell you about types of films you could make with varying numbers of people and of different sexes.

itself, then I would point out that asking a person with whom you are not already in a trusting relationship, could well lead to them running a mile at the mere mention of a video camera. Bear in mind that people are very conscious of the media and the risk of being 'caught out' on camera doing things they would rather not be seen doing. Whether it is hidden cameras, CCTV or home videos, we are all well used to having a laugh at another's expense. So ask yourself this: if someone you met at a party had the idea to get down and dirty in front of their video camera, would you jump at the chance? (Bearing in mind that you may never choose to see each other again.) The thought of a video somewhere out there with you rolling around naked could haunt you for a very long time, especially if you hadn't given thorough consideration to the consequences beforehand. Only once you have really addressed any concerns you might have will you be truly free to express yourself and to experiment on film. (See also pages 14–15 on how to protect yourself legally.)

If you have a partner with whom you would like to make a film and you are now both reading this book, then you are already halfway there and you can probably skip the next section – but for the rest of you...

HOW DO I APPROACH MY PARTNER WITH THE SUBJECT?

Be honest with yourself before going to your partner and it will save a lot of embarrassment later, and it can also be enlightening.

Do you feel that your partner would be *at all* interested in making a film together? As with most things, the best way to convince someone of an idea is by encouragement and complimentary support. The worst thing you can do is say that you want to try filming because you are bored of your sex life (however true this may be), or make the other person feel inadequate by comparing them to someone else. Be sensitive and don't forget

Don't just think about it – give it a go!

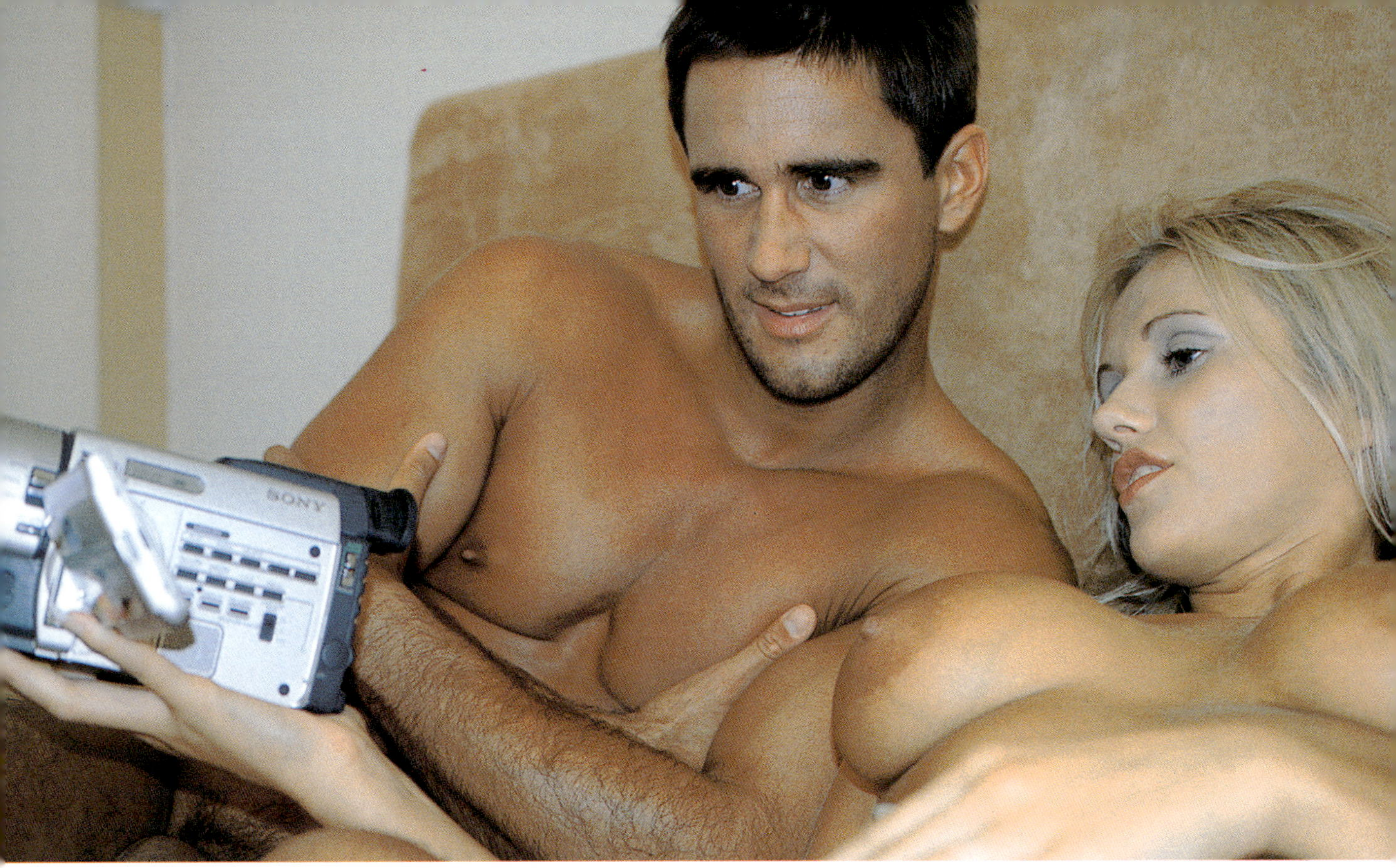

You may be critical of parts of your body that your partner really likes. Take them at their word.

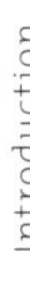

that coercion is extremely unethical, and there are laws against it.

If your relationship is such that sex is a difficult subject to broach or has historically caused you much upset, then jumping in at the deep end and suggesting you make a porn movie together may not be the best idea. I would certainly not encourage people to use this experience in the hope that it will be some sort of tonic for a failing relationship. A lot of people introduce the use of porn into their sex lives, whether by watching it or shooting it, as a means of kick-starting a flagging libido. The difference is that they still have feelings for each other and enough faith in the relationship to think it's worth investing some time in. Porn should never be used in a couple's relationship as a replacement for communication; this can only lead to more distance. It happens to all of us, after the initial boom in our sex life as a new couple, that when you are getting to know each other there is the almost inevitable decline into mediocre sex. But remember that you both have a responsibility to make an effort – and it can very much feel like an effort at first – to add spice to a sex life if you want to revive the energy you once had. Unfortunately you can't buy sex in a bottle, only lubrication.

Generally, when people are honest with themselves, they are not 100 percent proud of their physiques or performances and there is something about a camera lens that makes people instantly think 'magnifying glass'. If you are reading this as a woman who is interested in getting her man to perform a little better, bear in mind that when a man is not totally comfortable with the idea – especially when it comes to sex – it is much more obvious than with a woman. A woman can hide her nerves from the camera more effectively. So I would suggest that it is far better to approach the subject as an idea for an experiment, a bit of fun, an opportunity for adult play and exploration. You can even start from the standpoint of mocking the acting in real porn films, saying perhaps you could both do better. You never know, you might be able to.

It is very important that the two of you trust each other. Which is, strangely enough, why I suggest you both take the time to read and sign the agreement on page 15, keeping a copy each, so that you can both forget about it and move on to the next stage.

SEEING YOURSELF NAKED ON VIDEO FOR THE FIRST TIME

Ever heard your recorded voice played back to you? And have you ever met anyone who likes the sound of their recorded voice? Most people shy away from hearing themselves on tape and it can be the same with video.

It is almost inevitable that when you play back the videotape of the two of you getting down to it, you will see parts of your body at certain angles that you won't like, especially if they are badly lit. The important thing to remember is that this is true of even the most 'perfect' body. In my experience as producer, director and editor, I frequently have to edit out or 'cut' shots simply because, for one reason or another, the star does not look his or her best. However, this would not prevent me from hiring that model again; I would just have to re-think how that person should be filmed (maybe from a different angle, with an alternative lighting set up, or in different clothes).

You may find yourself being critical of parts of your body that your partner does not agree are unattractive. Take them at their word! Before you even thought about making this film, you were sleeping with each other, and your partner has seen seen all of you, every blemish from every angle (however much you tried to hide it), and they are still with you, so they must not mind it too much! Beauty is in the eye of the beholder, and you cannot assume that just because you don't look like the catwalk model considered to be the epitome of beauty in the Western world, any person with you is just being polite. I can tell you for a fact that there is a market for all shapes and sizes in the huge world of porn and a great deal of money is made from selling non-'catwalk model' type videos.

It's important to point out that natural 'off-screen' sex doesn't look like the highly polished high-budget porn/glamour shots, which are prevalent in videos and magazines. Nor should it. Much as this look has its place and can be extremely erotic, it is not the only way to present porn – in fact, in terms of volume of production, it isn't even the most popular. As a director, I think a natural performance by an ordinary-looking person is far sexier than that of a stereotypical 'mannequin'. It is perfectly natural and desirable to look flushed and sweaty, to screw your face up during orgasm and so on. It's what makes you a 'real' sexually attractive person, so go with it. After this film, hopefully you will have a record of your glory for future reference.

Your confidence in your body will grow as you explore and get used to seeing yourself on film.

A WORD ABOUT LEGALITY

Different countries have different ideas about freedom of expression and the role of the censor. Some have outlawed porn completely, while others openly embrace it. If you are thinking of making your film in a country that has very strict rules regarding pornography, then I suggest you read up on the specific laws applicable to that country.

The history of porn censorship illustrates clearly that the attitude to freedom of expression and censorship of sexual material is subject to change, and that the reasoning behind regulation is subject to fashion. The trend for an increasing tolerance towards sex and, more relevantly, towards sex on film, can change when a new government is elected that is less keen on freedom of choice than the previous administration.

This book is itself proof that we are all becoming more open about our interest in porn and are less ashamed to talk about it. Ten years ago such a book would probably not have existed publicly, but in the past decade couples have started to embrace pornography and erotica as never before. It is also a victory in the fight by women to be accepted as equals in every way, including sexually. Women no longer have to be told that any interest in sex or porn is wrong.

It would take another book to outline all the different laws of each country regarding the sale and distribution of porn, but it's useful to point out some general areas that you should be aware of, so that you can keep yourself on the right side of the law.

There are three main legal areas which you have to consider when making an erotic movie.

Consent

Obviously, any erotic movie is affected by all the usual laws regarding consent of either party, including those protecting you against assault, but it is also worth remembering that when professional producers make a porn film they get models to sign an Artist's Release form.

Both parties must consent to the sexual intercourse taking place. Failure of one of the parties to consent to the sexual intercourse may result in the other party being criminally charged with rape and/or assault. In addition, both parties must consent to their being filmed. It may be illegal for a party to be filmed without their knowledge. Consent must be given by both parties each time that they are filmed and consenting to being filmed once does not mean that the party has given their consent to being filmed on another occasion. An Artist's Release form legally gives the producer ownership rights of all the 'rushes' – the unedited film – and also agrees the rate of pay for the model. Without one of these, the producer cannot legally sell on the tape to distributors. So with reference to the film you are about to make, it is comforting to know that neither of you can sell or in any way make money out of the film, by giving a public viewing, for instance, without a signed release form from everyone involved. However, this restriction does not preclude free distribution – on the web, for example. Releasing a film without obtaining signed release forms only becomes illegal when there is money involved.

The consent form included in this book is not the same as the Artist's Release form mentioned previously. What the included consent form does is to point out and clarify for the two of you (or however many you decide to have in your video) that you own the rights to the video equally and cannot publicly display or sell the tape without all parties' signed permission. All this form does is echo the existing laws and clarifies them for you. It is always good to get a signed agreement rather than a spoken one so that you have something to which you can physically refer in order to safeguard against future misunderstandings. You have these rights anyway, so don't panic if you lose the paper or don't sign it.

Distribution

In most countries there are accepted and legal guidelines within which the porn industry is allowed to distribute and sell, and ways that it is not. This area is a legal minefield, especially as many governments prefer to keep it a grey area so that they can decide each individual case on its own circumstances. Fortunately the only thing that you need to consider with your film is that it may well be illegal to send your tape through the public post or to export/import it across any

national or state boundaries. There have been documented cases where customs officials have refused to believe couples who claim that the videotape they are carrying is for personal use only and not for sale. Any commercially available DVD or video has to go through the censors of that specific country to be classified according to its content. If you transport your work without going through this procedure, it may get treated as unclassified and therefore as an illegal film.

Public indecency

There are laws, as mentioned earlier, that also refer to public spaces and bodily exposure. In most countries you can be arrested simply for being nude in public, let alone having sex. Also many private companies and organizations may get upset if they see you filming on their property, and they have the right to stop you and to remove you from their premises – even if you are fully dressed.

But, these guidelines apart, as long as you are not selling your tape you are generally free to make your film and enjoy it.

Legal agreements

No matter how well you and your partner or partners think you get on, I advise that you sign a consent form before you begin. Type up the agreement below and print out a copy for everyone to sign. Make sure everyone has a fully signed copy. If you are involving others who will have an active role in the making of the movie, they too should have a copy of this agreement.

Consent Form

In consideration for each party agreeing to make this video [insert working title of film here] the parties agree that any performance that the parties make shall be owned by them in common (rather than jointly) with ownership split equally between them.

The sale, lending, renting or public airing in any way is forbidden without the prior written consent from all parties. For the avoidance of any doubt the parties agree that this agreement is legally binding.

....

....

[Printed names and signatures of everyone involved]

You, too, can be a porn star. In your own film you can become your fantasy ideals.

Fantasy and Role-play

Most people, especially women, have sexual fantasies of one kind or another. But it is common for people to lack confidence in expressing them, or to not realize what their fantasies are. This is normal. Being able to talk about fantasies takes practice. The more you try, the easier it becomes to express them.

Let your imagination act out situations to find answers and experience desires.

Fantasy and Role-play

To talk about your fantasies means to use speech in sex, and for some this is difficult. A lot of people fear their fantasies, believing them to be abnormal or unacceptable (especially in the light of today's political correctness). Generally we are not encouraged to speak freely about such things, especially in public, but this doesn't mean you can't express your innermost imaginings to a partner in which you trust.

It is a widely accepted myth that the fantasies that you wish to role-play in your sex life reflect the 'real' you. Fortunately, fantasy doesn't work that way. We fantasize about things we truly desire to happen, winning a million in the lottery, for example, but we are just as likely to fantasize about something that we truly would not want to happen because there are real consequences, responsibilities and other people and their reactions to be taken into account. The reason we imagine scenarios we don't necessarily want to happen is because the job of our imagination is to 'act out' situations as a way of finding answers to questions and experiencing desires. In this way we grow to know and understand ourselves better.

For example, a very publicly powerful person may well have fantasies of being subordinate to another, to help counteract the feelings of responsibility and stress experienced in their job. This is possibly why the tied-up politician scandals crop up every now and then.

Bringing authenticity into the film will make scenes more exciting to perform.

The role of fantasy

There is much misunderstanding about the role of fantasy in relation to a person's sexuality. A couple who like to dress up with the woman as a schoolgirl and the man as a teacher is a good example. You might think that the attractiveness such a couple would have for each other is based on child abuse or paedophilia.

Detail adds ambience and reality to the video, as these two examples show.

However, to see it this way is to miss a fundamental part of the scenario. The players know that they are in a fantasy environment, not normal life, and the age difference is not the attraction. These fantasists deny being interested in children, and there is no evidence to suggest any link.

The school uniform and ponytails are not typical of the wearer; they represent past times that were probably more carefree. This allows the wearer to act less responsibly, less like an adult, and that is the attraction. The wearer does not want to be younger, but wants to experience again a more innocent time and play out the fantasies she had towards older men at that age – the schoolmaster, the bus driver, and so on. It allows her to play out the normal fantasies she did not have the freedom to do at a pubescent age.

I'm sure, if you think about it, we have all re-played parts of our childhood in our minds, and not necessarily in a sexual way. It has a feeling of distance from where we are now, and because there is safety in the fact that the events of a childhood fantasy cannot actually be achieved, some people find the idea exciting.

I have spoken to many men and women about their fantasies, and the main difference between them has been that a man usually concentrates more on the person they are fantasizing about, especially their looks and their body, whereas women tend to take the whole scenario into consideration. For example, when I asked men what the room was like in their fantasy or what the model was wearing, or what had just happened before they met, the men often looked blank. For them it was a strange question. But women, on the other hand, found these questions far easier to answer and could often talk at length, stating to the last detail how their fantasy figure moved, what he said, what he wore and where they met.

I am always asking women about their fantasies, and something that has proved invaluable to me, and which I heartily recommend to others, is a women-only meal. My female friends and I started one every Wednesday evening a few years ago and called it the 'Shepherd's Pie Club'. We actually gave up the Shepherd's Pie pretty quickly, but we meet to talk about the week, give support to each other and get drunk. The conversation invariably turns to sex, so I often canvass my friends for ideas and ask them what they are into. The answers are varied, but the attention to detail is always there.

A theory is that women typically notice environmental factors as a result of the repression of fantasies through social stigmatization and guilt. If you keep a fantasy inside long enough, you have plenty of time to fill in the details. Intuitively I agree with this argument, and I also think that there is a surreal slant in the fantasies of some women.

By this, I mean that women often play with what is considered to be normal and decent social behaviour. Men do this too, but it tends to be more extreme with women. For example, my friend Jenny once told me the following fantasy that I really liked. She is at a masked ball 200 years ago, wearing a corseted dress and wig

but no knickers! Part of the evening's entertainment is a large banquet for all the guests. It is her job to be the first course, as it were. She sits on a chair with her legs spread wide open, held by two footmen. As the gentlemen enter the establishment and give their cloaks to the servants, they line up one by one and lick her out for a few moments until it is the turn of the man behind. The surrealism results from the apparent normality of being licked in such a grand social gathering. When Jenny told me this fantasy I could imagine the scene vividly. We agreed that how the scene was enacted was of the utmost importance, and it is also one of the hardest things to capture on film. But the answer is in the detail.

Similarly, when it comes to watching porn, one of the most common complaints I hear from women is about the styling. If the underwear, clothes or location is not to her taste, then a woman may not enjoy the scene. Even today, when I see a porn film for the first time, I can find my attention taken immediately by poor décor. In my films I always try to make the location at least interesting, if not always comfortable.

The Sub/Dom relationship

A fairly common fantasy is the Subordinate/Dominator partnership, or the fantasy in which you are made to have sex against your will, or with the slight twist of making someone else have sex against his or her will.

Whether it's a muscle-bound workman, a member of the armed forces, your favourite actor, a nurse or a female boss in stilettoes, many people imagine having their idea of the perfect physical manifestation of power overwhelm them, making them submit to whatever the figure wants and using them as a sex slave.

This is a very common fantasy, and in no way illustrates a lack of strength, maturity or judgement on the part of the host. Studies show that there is no one type of personality/situation that links fantasists. It certainly isn't gender specific. Both males and females are just as likely to be submissive or domineering, depending on their personality. I mention this because the myth that women are naturally more submissive is still widely accepted as truth.

This helps to explain what I have seen and experienced with regard to sexual Sub/Dom relationships. You only have to go to any sex club, or watch a Sub/Dom scene in a video, let alone experience the scene yourself, to see that subordinates can be very demanding.

Tried and tested fantasies, such as the French maid, are seen in rubber versions.

Jacques Lacan, a psychoanalyst from the 1960s who is still influential in his field, commented on the philosopher Hegel's 'Master–Slave' relationship. Hegel wrote that Western society sees power as domination and being on top, in whatever situation, with the result that the powerful is the more fortunate. What Lacan says is that this model is wrong. We should see Sub and Dom side by side, not one above the other. They work together symbiotically; that is, they are interdependent on one another. In terms of Sub/Dom relationships, the real power comes from the ability of a participant to access pleasure, and this can be either the subordinate or the dominator, or both.

A Sub very often defines the boundaries of what they will and won't do, giving advance warning of their 'safety word' – the word that tells the Dom to stop. Normally the phrases 'stop' and 'no, please don't' are part of the game, so another neutral word is agreed upon beforehand, which is used as a last resort. The Subs I have known have been no weaker in real life than the Doms. They are just as likely as the Doms to know what they want and how to get it, and as likely to be assertive in getting it.

So would you feel comfortable going with your submissive/dominating fantasies?

There are several key elements that make up a fantasy. You have aesthetics, location, role-play (including power play) and clothing and props, as well as the character you assume. The character you want to be can be anything from a tried and tested stereotype, such as a military officer and a gentleman or a famous person, or it can be as individual and specific as you wish. You could take elements of different people you have met or dreamed about and put them all together. But you have to know what you like in the first place.

Your fantasy persona doesn't have to be anything like the real, public you. In my films I believe a sense of reality is important in a fantasy, but this does not necessarily mean that your character has to be realistic and three-dimensional.

You can be whatever you want. Like a writer, you have all the freedom you allow yourself to have. You don't have to be your real age and social group, be living at this time in history or even be your real sex. You can direct the scene exactly the way you wish, with no need to justify the likelihood of this fantasy ever happening in real life. You and your partner do not need to be socially compatible in a situation – for example, you can have a sailor who happens to bump into a high-powered businesswoman, or an alien that lands its spaceship in the local convent.

A lot of people like to play with religion or tradition when fantasizing. I was never brought up to be religious and have tried to see the attraction, but it doesn't have the same effect on me as it does on others. There's no doubt that some people get a real kick out of the idea of sinning and redemption. The mere sight of a ceremonial gown or a confession box can send some people absolutely nuts.

What if you don't know what you like?

I think it is important, at this stage in the book, to think about how the reality of having choice can at times make us feel completely at a loss. It is a fact that a lot of people, especially younger readers, may not have a very developed sense of their own fantasies. Others might feel that reality does not always offer them the kick they need, but they feel bewildered when it comes to forming or developing even a small fantasy, and this they see as a lack of imagination.

However, the imagination is like a muscle. It needs a good 'work-out' regularly to achieve its full potential. If you don't exert it, it becomes flaccid. It is ironic in modern society, where choice is so revered and so wide ranging, that you could end up with an underdeveloped knowledge of what you really desire. The freedom to choose and the range of choice have almost become burdens. Worse still, choice can make you feel that you have to try everything out before you can relax and enjoy what you have discovered about yourself and your relationship. Don't fall into this trap! Making an erotic movie with your partner is meant to enhance your sex life, not add more anxiety to it.

There are many sexual acts that I haven't tried, and would probably be interested in trying at a later date. But I don't do them now because I want to enjoy each stage of discovery in depth. I have tried a lot, and have enjoyed most of it, and I don't ever want to become despondent with sex – I like it too much. My advice is to take it at your own pace and only move on to something new when you no longer feel inspired by what you are doing.

While it's true that some people can only enjoy fantasies that are based on a sense of power being shared equally between both partners, you must be honest with yourself. Is that your head talking about how you like to be seen in real-life nonsexual situations, or is it truly a reflection of your libido?

The normally submissive French maid can also be played as a dominatrix.

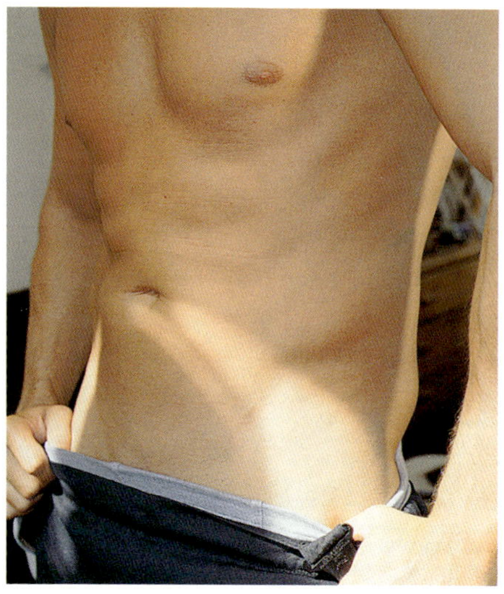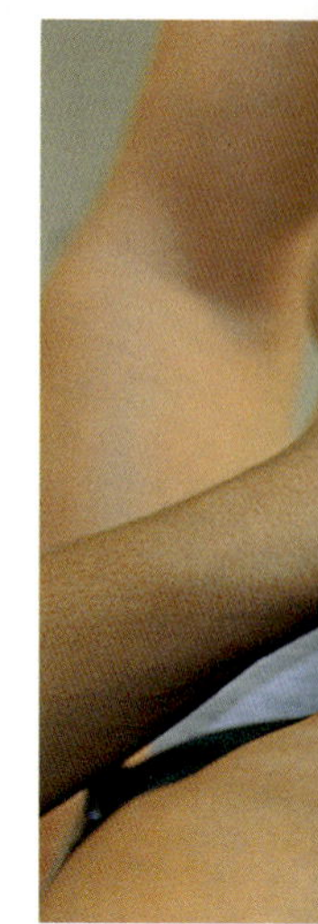

Remember that a trusting relationship should be enough for you to differentiate between these two, and to not feel ashamed. You will never reach your sexual potential unless you answer this question truthfully. Are you being polite with yourself? Are you afraid of your fantasy and where it will take you? If something turns you on, then it turns you on. Be honest. It doesn't hurt anyone, but I truly believe that lying to yourself can only be counter-productive and will inevitably result in a mediocre sex life. Both partners have a responsibility to be honest.

Whatever fantasy a man has, there will be professional videos, DVDs, magazines or websites to satisfy it. For instance, if he is turned on by big breasts then a sub-section will exist within each medium featuring big-breasted girls for him to choose from. Every preference in race, gender, age and appearance is catered for. There are tapes that are edited compilations of wall-to-wall hard-sex action with no story, and compilation tapes of scenes shot in public places.

The point is that the male-oriented sex market is made up of many genres and sub-genres, which have developed through years and years of choice and elimination. Pornographic magazines and films have been widely available since the 1950s, thanks to Hugh Hefner in the United States, George Harrison Marks in the United Kingdom, and Berth Milton and Alberto Ferro in Europe, to name but four. Men have had a long time to learn about what they desire sexually, whereas women are still developing their own sexual language. Porn made by women has only existed since the early 1980s when Candida Royale started making female-oriented erotica. So if you are a woman, don't think you are alone in feeling as if you don't know how to go about creating your first fantasy porn film. Practise makes perfect and practise is fun.

What fantasy would you like to explore?

A good way to start thinking about what fantasy you would like is to ask yourself how you want to feel or how you want people to react to you. Do you want them to adore you, to think you are stunning, powerful, unapproachable, talented, highly respected, sexy, brave, or maybe humble, pitied, used, useful, hard-working. Take this feeling as your starting point. Then ask what type of person epitomizes that feeling to you. If power is what you want to feel, then maybe a Supreme Court judge is your epitome of power. For some people the behaviour of the bossy woman at the local delicatessen is what they would like to imagine themselves to be. Maybe you see judges as having less power than a jury. It's up to you, and it needs to be personal to you to have meaning and be effective in pushing your buttons. So you have your character, now what?

What activity makes the most of your character's features? If it's a judge, then maybe condemning a criminal to hard labour is more evocative than sitting

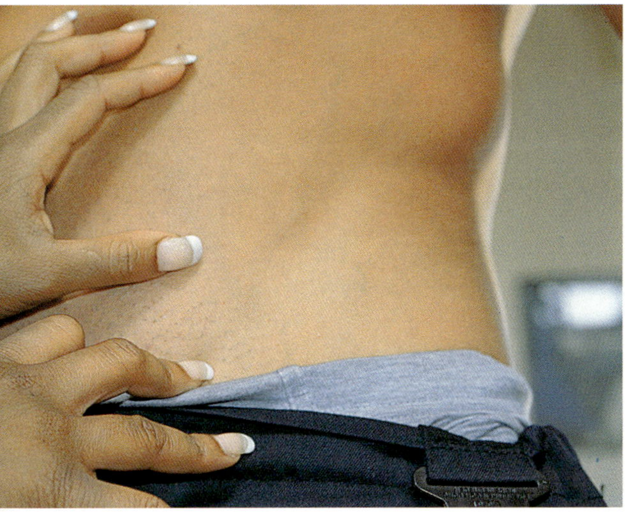
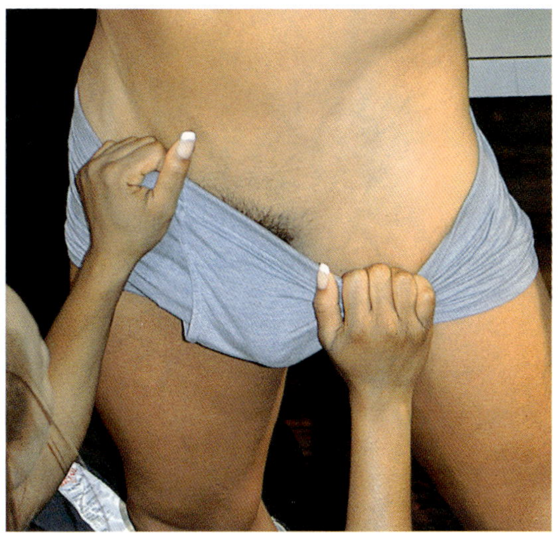

down discussing the possibilities of judicial reform with his/her peers. This seems an obvious point, but you should consider every aspect of the fantasy.

Then ask yourself: 'In order for my character to experience the feelings I want, what role will my partner need to play?' At this point we come across an important issue – that *your* fantasy may not necessarily be the same as your partner's. The way you deal with this will depend on how your relationship usually works. A good idea would be to take it in turns to try out each other's fantasies. But what happens if your partner asks you to do something you find abhorrent or morally wrong – should you go ahead to keep them happy?

The important thing is the degree to which you are uncomfortable with their fantasy. If it is simply a case that you would feel self-conscious, you don't see the point or feel too lazy to make the extra effort, then maybe you need to look at how generous you are willing to be. Maybe your partner is signalling that they would like to try something to rekindle the fire of your passion.

If the idea of your partner's fantasy makes you feel cheap or angry, then these are reactions that can be dealt with by open communication. Why does your partner want you to do this? Remember to listen patiently and don't base your opinions on generalizations of what is considered to be 'normal'. It may be that your partner's reasons for liking the idea are not what you fear they are, and maybe your fears can be overcome by open discussion

of both your beliefs. A lot of women are angered by pornography because we still live today with the legacy of the 1970s when we were categorically told that men sexually objectified women in order to subjugate them. Thankfully, the argument has moved on and now women are more accepting of the notion that to sexually objectify is human, and we all do it to varying degrees.

At the end of the day, sexual fantasies are often defined by the stresses and strains of a person's everyday life and their perceived position in the world outside the bedroom. Everybody has their personal preferences. What you have here is an opportunity to learn more about each other, if you choose to be supportive. And it is a dear thing to share because it requires complete honesty.

Role-play has been used a lot to help people understand situations, whether it is in a teaching facility or psychotherapeutic sense. It seems that acting out is invaluable in some contexts. However, the role that your partner asks you to play and whether you feel happy to fulfil their request is likely to reflect in some way your relationship, and you will instinctively know the value of this. So if, for example, your boyfriend is calling you all sorts of derogatory names, or asking you to act like a prostitute, you will know whether or not he treats you with respect in the rest of the relationship, and whether the role-play is an innocent area of fantasy.

Are you being polite with yourself? If something turns you on, then let yourself enjoy it.

But what if you both want to be on top?

I think the answer here is to take it in turns, not just for the sake of fairness. Sub and Dom are two sides of the same coin, and experiencing the other side can also give you pleasure, ideas, or even frustration that you can learn from and try out next time it's your turn. Failing that, I heartily recommend some form of wrestling.

Still in the dark?

If you are still having problems outlining your fantasies, then try working backwards, and start by defining what you definitely know your fantasy is not. Use the list of fantasy figures and their counterparts or opposites shown below, and cross through those that are a definite turn-off for you.

Types of fantasy figures and their opposites:

Sub	Dom
Soldier	Enemy
Slave	Master
Secretary	Boss
Criminal	Judge
Victim	Criminal
Student	Teacher
Patient	Nurse
Fan	Popstar
Dog	Owner
Chauffeur	Star
Criminal	Police
Small man	Giant woman
Horse	Rider
Patient	Doctor

Notice how some of these examples can be switched to be either Sub or Dom. This depends on the way you want to play them; in fact, nearly all of them could be switched.

For various reasons, some people find a sexually confident partner too demanding. This

Women and men on top

In the early 1990s, Nancy Friday published two books, one entitled *Women On Top* and the other called *Men In Love*. In these books she published excerpts from letters sent to her over a period of ten years in answer to adverts she placed in the 1980s. These letters told of a wide variety of both women's and men's fantasies. They included the gamut of the human sexual imagination, from some slightly less than legal acts, right through to monogamy with their existing partners! The range was large and inclusive, and the fantasies themselves were fascinating. Nancy assured her contributors that she would not criticize them on moral or ethical grounds, and the freedom with which they expressed their fantasies reflected this.

is a tricky situation to deal with, and it is one that I occasionally come across when I interview men. I still find the odd individual who can't even relax enough to let a woman go on top during sex. Some women I have spoken to have also had problems with partners who are extremely demanding about their sexual needs. This raises huge issues about whether they are willing to accept you as you are, and even whether they are attempting to suppress your development.

The fears experienced by some people with regard to having a sexually confident partner are generally to do with losing control. The irony being that when you relinquish control you often gain more power. Some people fear that an assertive partner may start to demand everything in the relationship. In my experience, sex can go a long way to smoothing over other disagreements, and knowing that you take pleasure and the time to please them can give your partner the peace of mind that he or she is respected and cared for.

Bear in mind that you are both trying to get to know each other, and that along the way there will be occasional stabs of jealousy and fear, especially if you are talking about other people, including ex-partners.

If you turn your back on learning about each other's more personal desires then you are left with only your idea of what your partner wants, which can create more problems than sitting down and discussing it openly.

The human imagination, by its very nature, paints pictures of extremes, and what you think may happen is usually a far cry from what does in fact happen when you are perfectly honest with each other about your desires. Besides, if the two of you reading this book together, you both share at least one fantasy – you both want to be porn stars!

Threesomes

Having sex with more than one person at a time is a common fantasy. In pornography this is group sex, but technically it's known as troilism, from the French word for three, *trois*. You can do this with your partner and another person, or you can join a group of swingers who meet regularly in your local area. Do not fear, there will definitely be a group of like-minded adults in your neighbourhood who are willing to take turns in each other's houses – or do fear, as the case may be.

I think it is fairly natural to want to try having sex with more than one person at a time, seeing as how we all have multiple sexually excitable orifices and sensitive spots. But you definitely need to talk the idea through with your partner if you are in a steady relationship, as you don't want to get a nasty surprise when some stranger turns up on your doorstep one day. It is a pretty potent thing, either good or bad, to see your partner having sex with someone else. I discuss how to use a camera with more than two in Chapter 5, 'Getting Going'.

FETISHES

While many of us like to entertain ideas of subordinate and dominator role-plays, probably including a little bit of dressing up, there are some people whose tastes are a little more peculiar or specialist. In recent years we have heard a lot about sadomasochism and other fetishes. There are now many fetish sex clubs in major cities all over the world, which are host to a whole range of identities and desires.

A few years ago I went to some of these clubs in London, and I was surprised by how many different fetishes there were that fell outside the normal sadomasochistic categories, and also by how few people were having any sort of sex in the sense of genital arousal and penetration.

To give you a few ideas, here is an outline of some of the more unusual practices that I came across. I would point out that some of these activities could be a little dangerous and should be approached with care if you wish to try them. You should also consider your physical fitness for some of the activities.

Human ponies

Visiting one London sex club, I met several people dressed up in bridles with leather and metal bits between the teeth, often wearing full horse's heads and hooves specially made to fit. They moved around the club in a horse-like manner, trotting forwards and backwards, raising their heads when their master made them halt, and generally having trouble negotiating spiral staircases. The owner carried a whip to train the 'horse' to do tricks, and sugar lumps were given as rewards. Sex may or may not occur between master and horse, depending on the couple. It is said that pony play, like other related fetishes, such as human piggies or puppies, has nothing to do with real-life bestiality as it is the role-play element that is the turn-on, not the 'love' of animals.

Giant women

Some people desire either to be very tall, to be over-powered by a very tall woman in high heels or to be a man in boots. Although you can't make yourself a hundred metres tall, you can suggest it. You can re-enact a 'Gulliverian' fantasy with a miniature doll; get a woman to walk all over you in high heels, 'trampling' you underfoot; or have your man tower over you naked. Photos for this genre are often taken from the ground upwards to create an exaggerated perspective of the body. Some people combine this fantasy with foot fetishes.

Balloon fetish

A model friend called Chanta told me that she often got paid simply for getting dressed up in costume, blowing

fights, but fans of sploshing also masturbate to pictures of women covered in cold baked beans and multicoloured paint. It seems that the idea of getting messy is what turns these people on. Getting soaked with water is also in this category, and it can be erotic, especially if you are fully dressed. It is sexy to see a clothed body becoming an exposed body with nothing actually having been taken off.

Fat admiration

Most people like to keep an eye on their weight in order not to get too fat. However, this is a handicap to anyone involved in Fat Admiration. The fatter the better, the bigger the more beautiful. With its curves and folds, some believe the fat body is more individual than the perceived svelte beauty of the supermodel. Fat fetishists strive to gain hanging and bulbous flesh, trying to increase their weight, often with the guidance of an established fat person. I've seen an illustration of two fat people with the man's erection rolling between their stomachs, that looked quite sensual, and I can see the attraction of soft, cuddly flesh. It is often men of small stature that enjoy this, possibly indulging in the idea of getting lost in their partner's body.

Foot fetish

This very popular fetish has almost become mainstream in recent years, often being featured in magazines and movies. Many men have taken quite an interest in female shoes and feet, licking and smelling them, and paying lots of money for old tennis shoes on the Internet. Moreover, you will often see images of women licking their own feet, or legs and feet being the focus of images in many nonfetish porn magazines.

Sports and shorts

With this fetish, groups of gay men wearing football (soccer) colours convene on special evenings. I find the sight of so many men hanging out by the bar wearing full kit including big socks and football boots, in an otherwise normal nightclub with strobe lighting and so on, is quite amusing, especially when they have to walk round with their wallets in hand. I haven't heard of any straight Sports and Shorts clubs – I think maybe because generally women are slightly less football mad on the whole.

No matter how strange you may think your fetish is, there will be others who share your fascination.

up balloons in front of her clients and popping them by sitting on them and bouncing up and down until they burst, or deliberately popping them in her face. Balloon enthusiasts, known as 'looners', also enjoy bouncing up and down on the balloons or rubbing balloons between their bodies during sex. Often 'looners' are also into rubber fetishism.

Sploshing

This involves getting messy with various foodstuffs, paints and mud. Many of us have seen women having mud

The resurgence of foot fetishism is thanks in part to the unique work of photographer Elmer Batters from the 1950s–70s. A compilation of his photographs was published in the 1990s. If you haven't seen his work, I highly recommend it. Even if you are not so keen on feet, his cheeky eroticism is rare in its vitality and sexual tension; it is full of images of women in torn stockings and close-up shots of their perfectly manicured feet, all taken at a time when everybody else was breast-fixated.

BDSM – Bondage and Discipline, Sadism and Masochism

BDSM is the term given to many types of sexual fantasies that are concerned with dominance and submission. The players take on previously agreed roles and play out their fantasies within consensual boundaries, which encourage a safe and respectful environment in which to explore their tastes. Many of the elements that make up BDSM I have already outlined, but BDSM is a matter of degree and many BDSM fans like to take it a little bit further.

I have spent a few wayward evenings visiting sex clubs and watching what goes on – from a *purely professional* point of view, you understand! There are usually areas where people can choose to be tied up on a variety of equipment and whipped, or possibly have pegs clipped to their privates, which are then twisted. Some of the participants are dressed in various uniforms or outfits: a middle-aged man in nappies (diapers), say, getting punished by a Femdom – female dominatrix. BDSM is about exploring trust, and emotional and psychological areas that straight sex (Vanilla Sex, as it is known) arguably does not. But it requires a certain attitude to be effective.

The more extreme sex acts tend to happen in smaller, more personal environments, like prostitutes' dungeons or people's homes. Such acts involve stronger corporal punishment, including branding, cutting or acts of extreme humiliation, like showers of every type of human excretion. The most extreme acts are referred to as 'Edge Play', where players push the envelope of safety and consent. Acts such as auto-asphyxiation or in which bodily fluids are exchanged are very rare but they do exist.

One point I want to make here is that if you find something really abhorrent or upsetting, you owe it to nobody to put yourself through it. If you feel unsafe, or if the practice brings back bad memories, then you are entitled to say 'no' and mean exactly that without your partner having to completely understand your reasons. You should not feel like a killjoy. I have fantasies about many different scenarios and have engaged in partners' fantasies which I have either enjoyed or not, but there are things I won't do for anyone. You can always find something else to do instead. From a legal point of view, anyone who is restrained during sex must have consented to being restrained and must be released immediately upon their request. Restraining someone against their will is illegal and will qualify as assault and unlawful detention (see also pages 14–15).

Bear in mind that somebody who knows what they like and is trusting enough to be able to ask for it is much more attractive than someone who waits in the wings for another person to tell them what to do. This is true even of subordinates, who naturally have a desire to be bossed about. If you know what you like, be assertive. Tell your partner what you want them to do; don't expect them to read your mind. Have the conversation so that you can get started and begin to build on your relationship and extend yourselves. Get the words out the way so you can start to play. Do it now!

These days many non-fetish magazines also contain shots that focus on women's feet.

Setting the Scene

Preparations for your porn movie depend on what you plan to do. If you want to film you and your partner having sex, you only need to think about make-up, a little bit of clothing and location. But if you plan to enact your favourite fantasy, then there is a lot more specialist equipment and props you may need to consider.

There are a million different looks and characters you can create.

Setting the Scene

Contrary to popular belief, if you are appearing in a porn movie you do not have to pile on the make-up, although you could be forgiven for thinking you do if you use most porn films as a guide. There is a tradition for heavy make-up in the porn industry because the idea of getting totally tarted up is one thing people enjoy. It can add excitement, especially if you usually wear very little – and there is a lot to be said for the cheap and sluttish look.

MAKE-UP AND BODY IMAGE

If this is the look you are after, then the way to it is very simple. Just put more make-up on, especially lip liner, which should be drawn just outside the actual edge of the mouth to emphasize the shape. This achieves that 'collagen injection' look, otherwise only possible with painful beauty therapies or by eating a whole bucket of salt popcorn. Everybody can see that this is not your real lip line and that's the fun of it. So, if you like this instant 'trash' look, go for it!

There are fashions in porn make-up as with any other style. Sometimes a lot of models wear an over-lip line with natural fleshy colours, almost to make the lips look like a pouting vagina, while their foundation is extra matt, usually of a honey/peach colour.

Glitter can be popular because it works well in bright lighting. Eyeshadow colours vary, but lilac/purple and brown are often used together. You can also buy wigs, including pubic wigs, in all shapes and sizes.

Men in mascara

Personally, I really like to see men in full facial make-up too. I like eyeshadow, eyebrows, cheeks and lipstick – the lot! It's only recently that this idea has become unpopular. Back in the 1970s there was David Bowie and Iggy Pop, in the 1980s pop idols like Adam Ant, and more recently, Eddie Izzard. The most popular photo of Kurt Cobain from rock group Nirvana is the one where he is wearing black eyeliner. Men are still men with makeup, and women fall over themselves for them – so think about it.

Try out 'trashy' make-up. Looking and feeling cheap might be just the thing that gets you going.

If you do try it, I suggest you get a woman to apply the make-up because for some reason men just can't do it without a lot of practice. It's also a lot of fun putting make-up on your man if you have never tried it before. Interestingly, if you get drunk with your friends, I bet that a lot of them admit to trying out make-up on their boyfriends, so it is obviously some sort of secret pastime for a lot of couples. Besides, seeing men in make-up reminds us women how pretty we are!

Professionally, I always try to use make-up that is appropriate in its context. I think it destroys the realism when a woman playing the part of a secretary appears in make-up she would wear when going out to a nightclub. In these two situations the make-up should be totally unique.

Try your man in make-up; he can be your rock star.

In my 13-part series called 'Planet Nadia', I supposedly followed a student called Nadia for 13 weeks, filming her in many situations. In one scene she arrived at her wholesome and healthy friend Nicola's house at 10 am, after a night out at a club. In the bright morning sun, the contrast between Nadia's clubbing clothes and make-up and Nicola's fresh-faced look succeeded in establishing their characters very quickly.

For the body, you can use many different products to make your skin appear irresistible on film. One of the easiest to find, and also one of the most effective, is baby oil. A small amount can give your skin a healthy glow which looks great. However, be sparing, as too much will make you look slimy, and slimy doesn't go well with sex.

Another great tip is to shoot your film a few hours after working out in the gym, as your skin will be tighter and your body parts will swing more attractively. This is true even for people who don't exercise regularly – for a few hours, at least, physical exercise lifts your muscles into a more pert position. Just don't over-do it.

Pubic trends

Since the mid-1990s women's pubic hair has been disappearing at quite a rate. Why? Well, this trend is rooted in contemporary politics. In the early 1990s, American laws regarding censorship were relaxed in line with the more liberal politics of the day. This meant that porn producers were allowed to show more on video. One of the traditionally censored areas of porn was the inner and outer labia (pink): there were limits to how much you were allowed to show, especially if there was movement! As the producers were given more rein, they naturally wanted to make the most of it, and encouraged porn stars to shave off more hair to make more flesh visible.

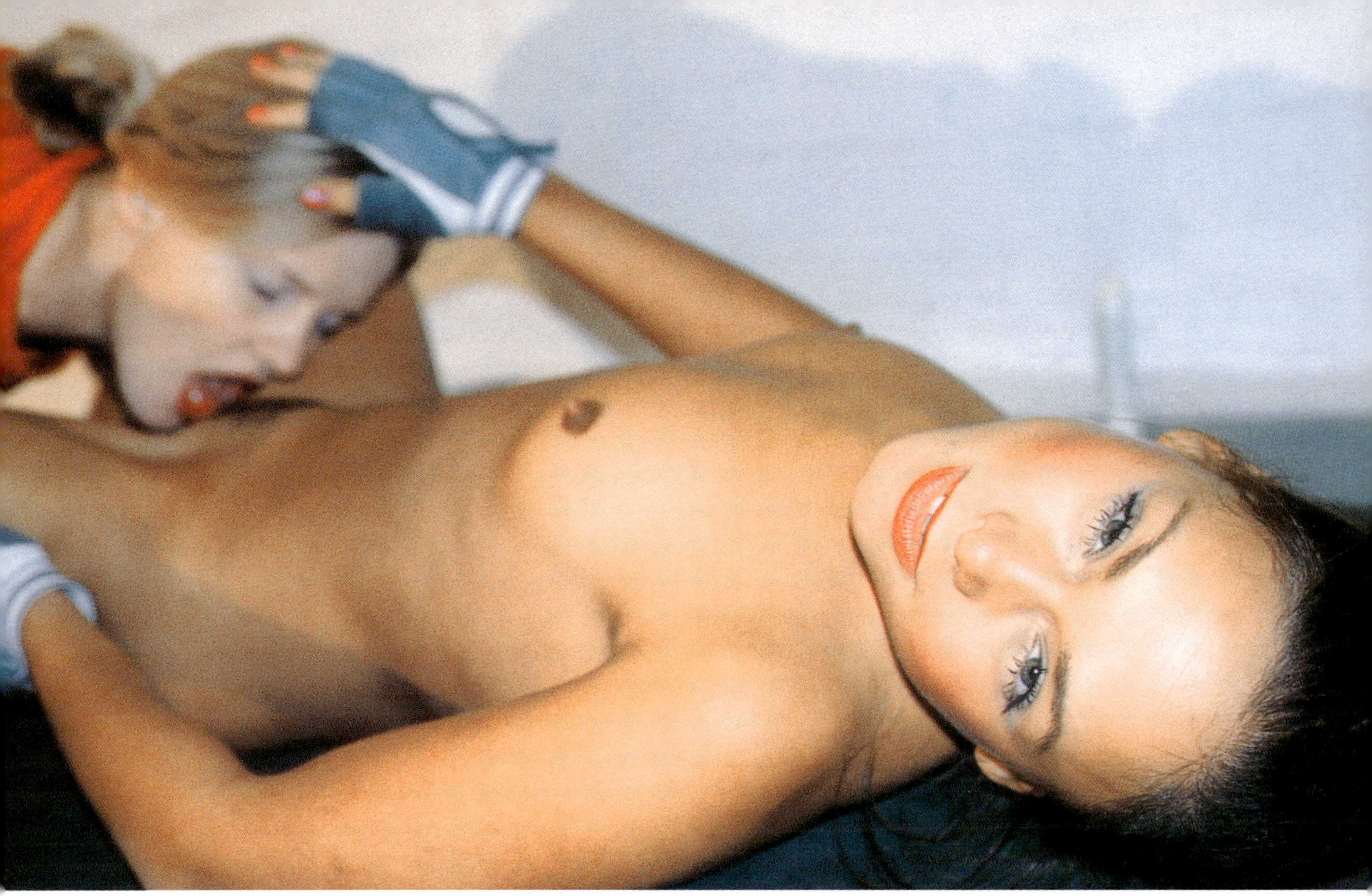

The pubic hair trend trickled down from porn videos to the streets as a fashion. It then came across the Atlantic to Europe and England, where censorship was much more stringent – until 2000 no hardcore films were allowed to be possessed, let alone made, in England. Ironically, producers had to censor even more due to the fact that, if you can't show all that much and you are filming a shaven woman, you aren't allowed to do close-ups. The more on display, the more has to be obscured by camera angles and so on. British censorship laws mean you have to perform all sorts of strange shots and edits, and they are a minefield if you don't know what you are doing.

But in pornography, the fashion is now moving back to hairier models – just as England caught up! Even so, the outer labia (lips) are definitely more sensitive to touch if they are shaven. You don't have to shave off the front at all, but give shaving underneath a try as it is really smooth.

COSTUME

Clothes are very important even if you only intend to take them off. What you wear is shorthand for what you think about yourself. Up to 70 percent of our first impression of someone will be based on what they look like.

During my research over the past five years into what makes men and women 'tick' sexually, I have uncovered several differences between what a woman wants in an erotic movie and what a man wants. One of the points that discouraged women from buying the traditional porn film was a lack of consideration about clothing. When women fantasize, they take into account the whole scenario. I found that the women I spoke to could describe what they imagined their fantasy man to be wearing, or what they themselves were wearing, down to the last detail.

Clothing can be one of the most erotic aspects of a porn movie, even when there is very little of it.

and top if the character requires it, and the obligatory glass high heels. For men, it's a tight T-shirt and smart trousers or suit, or handyman clothes. About 90 percent of porn films stick to these guidelines, and while I'm not saying they are unattractive, I do think that it could be time for change, and there is plenty of scope for you to play with.

However, using a porn uniform will give your film a certain feel. The reasons why this look is preferred are simple: bright pastel colours and silver make a body look more tanned than it really is; contrasting colours like black and red are striking and sensuous; and tight-fitting clothes give an idea of the body's shape before you unwrap it.

> Interestingly, there seem to be a lot of period narratives set in huge mansions with full period dress in Italian porn. When it comes to the sex, they keep their clothes on – all of them – only opening the man's fly, and pulling down the woman's top to reveal her breasts and lifting up the skirt to show penetration. The rest is nearly all out of sight. I have always thought that maybe they pay an awful lot for the costumes and want to make the most of them on screen, but surely it must cost far more in dry-cleaning bills!

What clothes turn you on? They may not be the standard porn uniform.

Men, on the other hand, could definitely remember fantasizing about women in specific types of clothes – stockings and suspenders, for example – but they didn't go as far as women. I have interviewed men who were completely lost when I asked them what their fantasy girl was wearing. Of course there are exceptions to the rule, but it seems that clothes are very important in sex, and the woman is more likely to be critical and selective about the clothes used in a porn film. Playing out your fantasy in your movie is discussed in depth in Chapter 2, 'Fantasy and Role-play'.

The porn uniform

There are a few typical porn uniforms. For women it consists of big hair and brash make-up, a tight-fitting, brightly coloured dress (preferably shiny), or a tight skirt

What you should be considering before you go jumping for the lamé, is what kind of feel you want these clothes to give you. Do you want to feel cheap, expensive, dominating, submissive, innocent? Will the clothes be dictated by the part you are playing in a fantasy? A French maid can only really wear a French maid's outfit. Personally, I really like the medical look – it gets me every time. But there are many different types of nurse's uniforms available, including real nurse's uniforms from a uniform shop, rubber ones or trashy nylon ones. Each will give a different feel to your film. There is definitely the correct costume for you, if you put the effort into looking around at what is available.

The usual tried-and-tested sexy clothes are all options: the combination of covered and uncovered skin that stockings and suspenders offer; the vulnerability and power of high heels; the soft feeling of silk against the skin for both men and women. For a woman to feel silk against a man's hairy skin can be very exciting. The contrast between his masculinity and the femininity of the silk actually makes your man seem manlier. It is only Western society that says men in dresses are peculiar; many other cultures accept it as normal. You may like to give it a try; it will at least be a laugh. Don't forget that some men like to see their woman in nothing but the man's work shirt, as it emphasizes her femininity.

while you are the innocent Catholic girl in pure white cotton knickers. All these characters need specific clothes to bring the fantasy to life, and planning what to wear and buying the clothes can be half the fun.

It is important to remember that you don't have to be politically correct with your choice of clothes or fantasy. This is an unreal situation; it doesn't necessarily represent what you want to happen in real life. And if you want outrageously sexy costumes, like crotchless basques or gimp outfits, there are stores worldwide and websites that stock and ship them in a just few days.

Discuss with your partner what they like. Even if it is not your favourite fantasy, or the idea makes you feel

Some people are sent wild by the feel of rubber or latex, others by uniforms. You should also consider whether the clothes are clean or dirty. Maybe a school uniform can be improved by adding grass stains to the knees or knickers. Maybe you are to be punished for not keeping your tennis whites clean. Maybe you are a scruffy hillbilly kid with straw in your hair and you are taken in by a voluptuous reverend's wife for a good scrub-up. Maybe you want your man to be the rough-and-ready type,

a little bit daft, the power of being the pleasure-giver can be immeasurable. Watching him or her melt under your control when you wear something that probably carries no significance for you, can give you even more power.

One important aspect to consider about clothes is how they fit in with your whole scenario, especially your location. A stark contrast works well: a policeman in

Enjoying the sensation of different materials on your partner's body can be a real turn-on.

Experiment with a range of household props, but be hygiene-conscious.

in themselves, but they add to the scene, which is especially important to women, I find. These little details can make a good sex scene great.

Try to use these props convincingly, if you can, although being a good actor has never been a prerequisite for a porn star. At the same time try not to nervously overuse your prop. How you wield a feather duster will make the difference between looking like a sexy little French maid or a clown.

If you have a specific plot, you will need specific props. For example, my first erotic movie was a medical drama set in a railway station. A woman had abdominal pains on the station platform and was in dire need of an internal examination, then and there from a doctor, who took out his leather bag, and put on a pair of medical gloves. He then took out various objects and set about treating the patient. As it was supposed to be comedic, I decided that the medical props would be something else entirely. I used a corkscrew as a speculum, with which the doctor spread the patient's legs and went about opening up her cervix – obviously not for real. But the comedic effect was achieved through the medical language used, the corkscrew and everyone's concerned appearance.

The second type of prop is the type for use on or in the body. Sex shops stock all types of equipment, from dildos and vibrators to cock rings, whips and lotions. You can keep yourself busy just trying out a new toy once a week. Sex shop toys have the appeal of being rather cheap-looking – they are usually made of plastic and cast in lurid colours, not to mention the veined flesh-coloured 'super cock' vibrators available. Their cheapness – in terms of look, not cost – can really add to your film, if that is what you are after.

When choosing a vibrator or dildo, bear in mind that there are many different shapes and sizes. No doubt you will have to try a few before you find one that suits you. One of the main considerations is the texture of the material it is made of – some are cast in rigid plastic and others are made of softer rubber. The wrong one can feel quite uncomfortable, so if you don't find the right one straight away, persevere. Some come with rotating internal pearls and external clitoral and/or anal

your home, for example, or a sailor at your office. The contrast of the uniform and the familiar environment can be fun. You can also create an effect by wearing opposite types of clothes: the woman dressed in a smart suit and lingerie, for example, while the man is a dirty refuse collector.

Props

There are two types of props you may want to play with. Firstly, you have the type of props that support your character – for example, a toolbox for a handyman, a pen and shorthand pad for a secretary, or a duster for a French maid. These props may not be sexually exciting stimulators. If you are put off by the realistic 'bulging vein' style of many dildos, you can buy ones shaped like dolphins and frogs – I don't know why manufacturers think we might be into frogs, but it takes all sorts.

Keep an eye out for props in places you wouldn't immediately consider. A trip to the supermarket can result in many discoveries if you think about objects in terms of their size, texture, shape and temperature, rather than for their usual function. I'm always keeping one eye out for new props to try out in films. Look at the products with a 'sexual eye'. The vegetable counter alone can keep you going for months! Think not only of the phallic-shaped vegetables like cucumbers, carrots and the like, but also of the textured vegetables, such as corn on the cob, which you can try gently rubbed on the clitoris. Another example of using a piece of fruit here is to take a bite from an apple and rubbing the moist flesh of the apple around the clitoris.

If you are using a vegetable, try gently heating it in a pot of boiled water, or cooling it down in the freezer for five minutes. Obviously, there are safety implications here! Don't heat vegetables directly in the microwave and don't boil them for longer than a couple of minutes. Also be aware of 'bits' of vegetable matter coming loose, so such vegetables are best not used internally. Also remember that vegetables have different textures and hardness. A courgette (zucchini) is much softer inside you than a carrot, and if the market for vibrators is anything to go by, some women prefer softer to harder.

You don't only have to use dildos or vibrators or vegetables internally on a woman or man – you can use other objects too. I've seen all sorts, from broom handles to pens. *But be extremely careful.* Avoid anything with removable parts. Also, anything with a concave end, that is curving inward, can cause internal suction, which can be very painful on the cervix afterwards. So be responsible when you are experimenting – after all, it's your body.

Spreads and oils

Other extras include spreads, syrups, creams and edible pastes. Chocolate spreads are a favourite. You can buy them in supermarkets

Go on and get fruity with your favourite produce.

Keep an eye out for props in places you wouldn't normally consider.

with a brush applicator. But be careful not to put on more than you can lick off, as it has very few other uses. It is easy to forget when you are getting someone to lick something off another's body that the 'licker' tastes and swallows it. I made that mistake with my first commercial porn programme, 'Eat Me/Keep Me'. After getting the lovely Majella and Nadia to lick cheese spread, trifle, maple syrup and dusted icing sugar off each other, and wash it down with beer, at the end of the shoot Nadia threw up, which wasn't exactly the desired effect.

> I don't know why cream is liked so much as a sexual stimulant. When I was 18, I tried it with my boyfriend on a romantic weekend away. I got all dressed up in a full basque, suspenders and stockings, but after ten minutes, our body heat started to make the cream smell decidedly cheesy. It was like trying to make love in a vat of Stilton (see Sploshing in Chapter 2)!

There is also the whole '9 ½ weeks' scenario – using the taste of food as both a punishment and a source of pleasure. It helps if you know what your partner loves to eat and what he or she can't stand, and don't miss out on the 'can't stand' food types. It can give you both hours of fun, but only if your partner is blindfolded. Remember the part with the hot chilli and milk?

Oils and moisturizers can feel really lovely, especially for massage, as this wakes the body up and makes it more sensitive, to even the slightest touch. But be careful not to get oil on the woman's vagina as it acts as a shield and actually lessens sensitivity.

It's a myth that a woman is ready for sex when she is 'wet' – it is actually just the first stage. If you carry on with foreplay, especially with internal masturbation, the vagina initially widens to allow penetration, but if you continue internally using a narrow dildo or just one finger, the vagina naturally narrows again, but giving the woman more stimulation. Similarly, if the woman gets no internal masturbation or foreplay, the initial penetration may feel tight because she hasn't opened up at all. But eventually it will loosen up more, and then the woman may feel less sensation because the internal walls haven't had a chance to 'feel' for the penis. For more about how to strengthen internal muscles, see the section on Positions in Chapter 5, 'Getting Going'.

Props of restraint, such as handcuffs, rope and scarves, can be used to tie up your partner and render them powerless to resist your demands. I talk about S & M and the equipment you may want to use, as well as its legalities, in Chapter 2, 'Fantasy and Role-play'.

CHOOSING A LOCATION

What does it matter where you film your sex scene? Well, for many people it does matter. Some people really believe it doesn't matter, until you show them how you can improve a film by changing the setting. On the whole, women take a lot of notice of the location, so for her alone, you should give it some thought.

Professionally, I have always taken the greatest care when choosing locations. To me, and to many other women that I interviewed and read about, a shabby or boring setting can 'break' a scene. I also look for variety, as I don't want to see the same places again and again.

As with costume, there is a set of typical porn locations. The selection ranges from the decadent Los Angeles house with marbled floors and swimming pool, to the glossy studio set-up, the office, the hotel room, and the outlandish fantasy scenario.

How do you choose your location?

If you are looking for a specific location, whether it is interior (anywhere with four walls and a roof) or exterior, here are some things you should think about.

Interior locations

People don't generally give it much thought, but different rooms have a range of associations because of their everyday uses. When thinking about choosing a location for your erotic movie, you have to refer back to your script and ask yourself what sort of scene you want. Creating a studio scene from scratch and making it convincing can cost a lot of money, but you can make your house the ideal location if you think about it first.

Does your story require a specific setting? For example, are you seducing the washing machine repairman? If so, the kitchen or utility room is probably best, providing there is enough room for the lighting, a cameraman and performers.

Do you want comfort, and what kind of sex are you intending to have? Different rooms have varying levels of comfort. The bedroom and living room are generally designed for relaxation, whereas the utility room and garage usually aren't. If you are planning to have long, sensual sex then lying on a large deep-pile rug in front of the fireplace or simply getting into bed is probably best

Think about how you want to have sex when you choose the room.

Almost every location you can think of has the potential to be the setting for your erotic movie.

because a setting it is more comfortable and allows you both to relax.

If, however, you plan to shoot quick sex, perhaps a one-night stand or an illicit encounter – between a boss and a worker, for example, or between two separately married individuals – then a 'make-do' location, like a hallway or broom cupboard, is best. It gives the idea of 'lustful impatience'. The cupboard implies secret, forbidden sex. Stairs and hallways imply a similar feeling, as well as incorporating the risk factor of being discovered.

Some people really like the idea of incorporating bathtime in their sexual fantasy, so a shower cubicle or bathroom might be your choice, allowing you to enjoy washing each other before moving onto the sex. Saunas are another favourite – there is something inherently sexy about bodies covered in beads of sweat, but be careful about getting the equipment wet.

If you have a loft or a cellar in your house, these can be evocative places to make a film. I once made a film called *Party 2001* about a couple who got locked in their cellar by accident just before a hundred or so of their friends arrived for a New Year's Eve party at their house. After the inevitable argument as to whose fault it was, they made up and had rampant sex among the broken bicycles and old boxes, both dressed up in their best clothes – for a few moments, anyway.

If you are a member of a swinger's group in which couples take turns in hosting the party, then you have many locations at your disposal. You can think about these different locations and the range of décor and types of rooms, in the same way as outlined earlier in this section. Try to make the most of the different moods of each house. Some are traditional, others might be country styled, and some contemporary and minimalist. Try to think about how the story might fit the location. You can sustain variety by using the setting as a restrictive rule that defines the film's energy or feel.

Maybe you know the owner of a shop or restaurant who would turn a blind eye for a few hours while you

film a couple having under-the-table sex. Maybe you can seduce the shop or restaurant owner – there's nothing like getting a good location and a good performer all in the same deal!

I have shot in many different locations because it is important to retain interest – both for the viewers and myself. I know I get bored of seeing sex shot in domestic environments all the time. Among other locations, I have filmed in half-derelict buildings, abandoned properties, cars, nightclubs and on fire escapes. Just make sure that wherever you decide to shoot, you have permission and the place is safe and secluded.

Derelict buildings and cluttered settings can add raunchiness and a sense of spontaneity to a scene.

If you are willing to ask around, there are often people happy to lend you equipment – even old buses – to help make your erotic fantasy masterpiece.

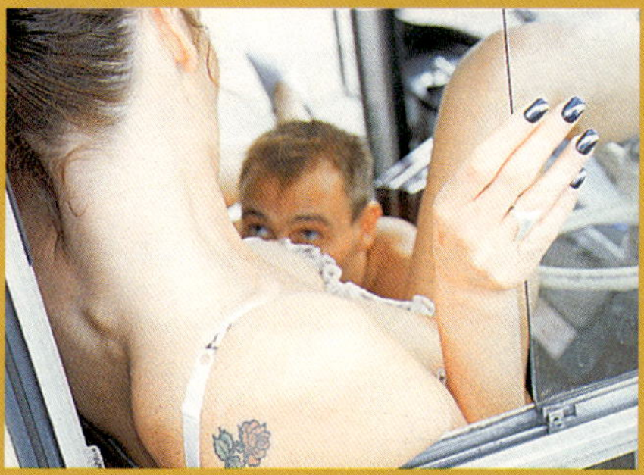

Exterior locations

As you can imagine, there are legal implications about shooting an adult film out in the open. Even filming a scene in your back garden, where you are the registered tenant or owner of the property can, in theory, still get you arrested for exposing yourself or carrying out lewd acts, so be careful. Basically, take every precaution to make sure that you cannot be seen from anywhere else.

Sometimes the risk of discovery is the 'kick'.

Public decency laws vary around the world, and in America they are different in almost every state. While in England engaging in sex in a place open to the public rarely results in prosecution, in some states in the US you can be imprisoned for up to three years for the same offence. In Australia the sentence is more likely to be about six months.

The message here, then, is basically to make sure that you know exactly what the penalties might be and how you can avoid them before you even think about getting naked in public.

A lot of adult movies these days are filmed outside in semi-secluded and sometimes public places. However this is not strictly legal, and if you are caught having sex or exposing yourself in public, you may be accused of a public order offence. When streakers run onto sports pitches we are all highly entertained, and most of us don't feel society suffers directly as a result, but the streakers are still arrested and ordinarily charged. Ultimately, you have to regulate yourself and decide just how much of a risk you want to take – which in itself can be a hell of a turn-on. I am just not encouraging you to strut into your local grocery store and get frisky in the freezer section. There, that's my lecture over.

In theory, if you intend to mount your camera on a tripod to film in a street as an introduction to your movie, even without filming any sex, you should get permission. The same rule applies if you use streets that come under the authority of a specific association. Generally, you shouldn't get into any trouble if you do not obstruct pavements (sidewalks) or thoroughfares; do not directly focus on any individual or passer-by; and are not obscene in any way. After all, tourists are always filming in the streets and they're always in the way, come to think of it.

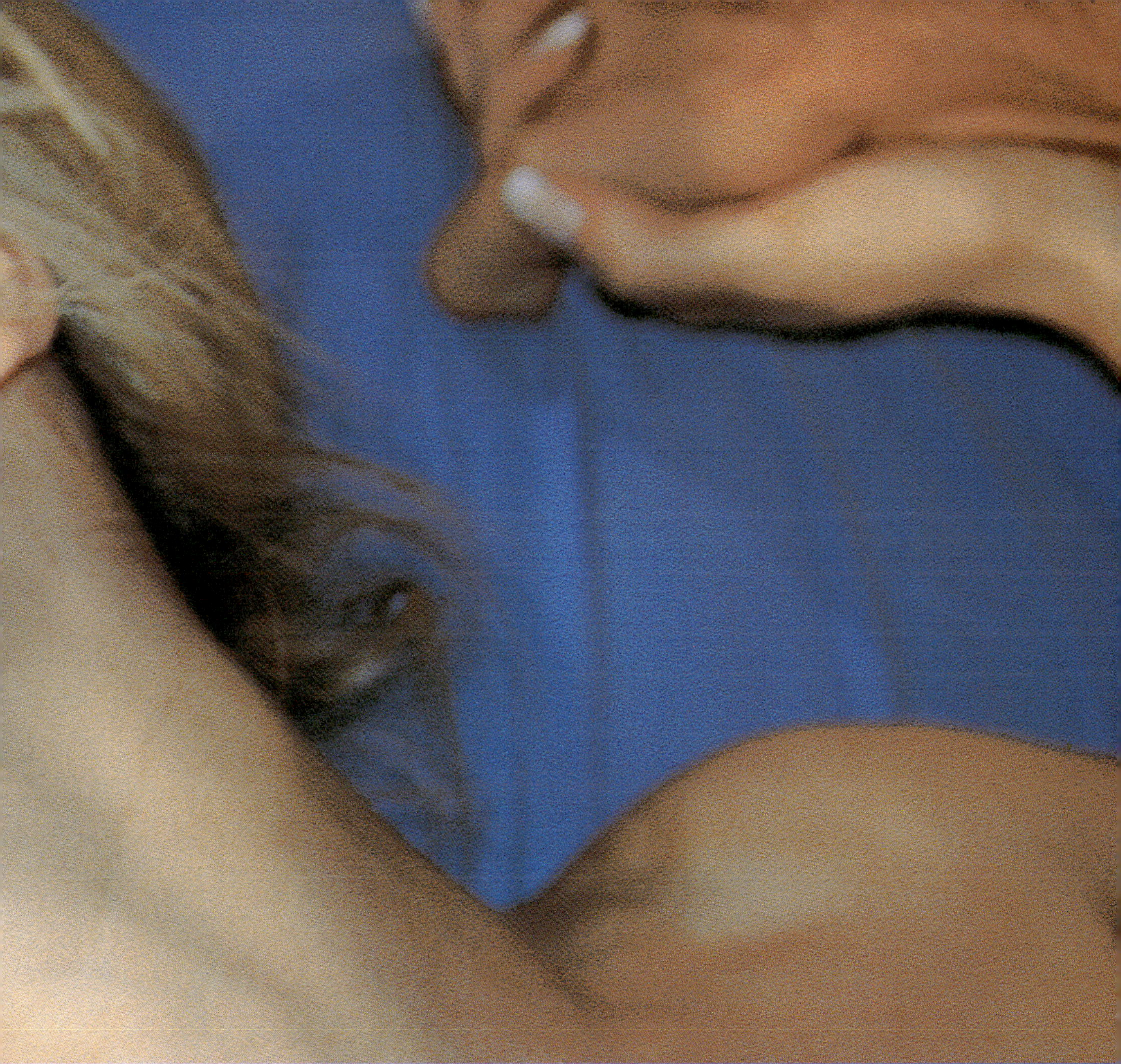

Planning

So, you have your characters, you know where you want to make your film, you've booked your costumes, and you have a variety of phallic vegetables in the refrigerator. What next? Now you need to work out just what sort of film it will be and how you are going to shoot each scene for the best possible results.

Let your instincts drive you, as the final result is for your enjoyment.

Planning

By now, you are probably dying to get on with the sex, but if you really want to make a movie that you will both love to watch over and over again, it's important to think ahead and plan what you want to film. Are there any parts of your body that you would rather not see in widescreen? Are there any camera angles that excite you? Now is the time to make those decisions.

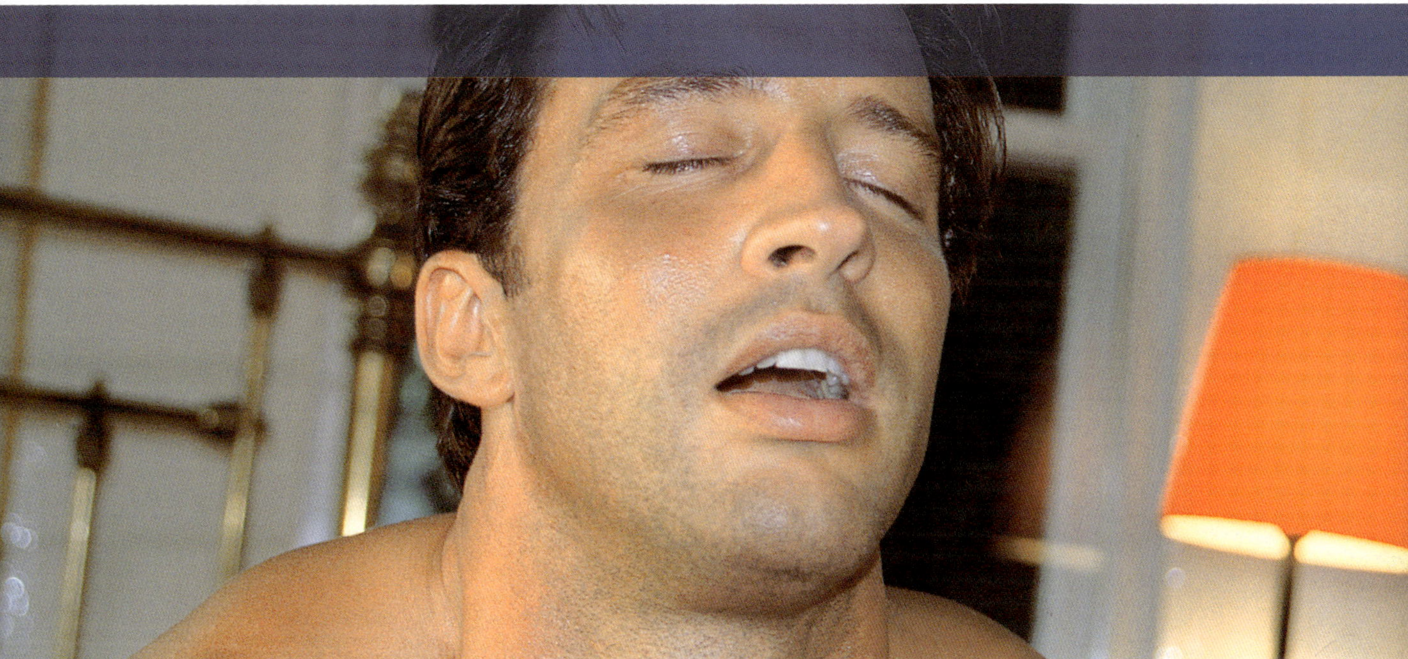

Whether you are just going into the next room to make your film, or if you have hired a mansion in the country, there are some essential items you will need to have with you:

- Script
- Storyboard
- Shot list
- Camera (see page 89)
- Tripod or equivalent (see page 94)
- Lights – two lower wattage and one higher wattage (see page 101)
- Stands for lights
- Clothes, make-up and props
- Toys and lubricant, if required
- Condoms
- Signed forms

THE STORYBOARD

Mainstream films have a storyboard created and worked out way in advance of the start of production. Often it is used to work out the expected costs in order to create a budget. It is also used by the crew as a base for any changes and to refer to as an agreed direction for the film. More importantly, the storyboard should reflect the order, variety and content of all the different shots throughout the film. Every change of scene, camera angle and focus should be shown on it. The director will use the storyboard to visualize and design the various shots with the technical staff, making sure that the desired shot is really achievable. Also, at this point, the decisions are made as to what type of shot is used, for example a pan with a

Imagine the different types of shots you want when planning your movie.

wide angle, or a medium-angle tracking shot ending close-up on the main character's face. The storyboard helps everyone involved, including performers and behind-the-scenes staff, to know exactly where they are and what is happening when.

A storyboard consists of an individual drawing of the intended framing and contents of each shot, and written underneath, descriptions of any camera movement and any cue lines – the first line a performer says. The point of the storyboard is to provide clarity and to ensure that all relevant staff are informed as to exactly what shot is coming up next.

I have to admit that I don't know many porn producers who sit down and work through the film they are about to shoot, shot by shot, drawing out the individual frames and writing down chosen camera moves (in fact, I don't know many porn producers that can draw). The reason is not simply a lack of professionalism or know-how. There are certain restrictions on the day-to-day organization and logistics of running a pornography production unit that make any type of rigorous planning quite difficult. Due to the unsociable image that adult movies still have, you can never really be sure if the location or staff and models you have booked will indeed be the very same ones you actually film come the day of the shoot, purely because people in the business often change their minds. The industry is always fluctuating and economics of the industry necessitate that shoots be done quickly, sometimes up to two scenes a day!

However, you can have all the preparation time you could wish for. You can create your own erotic movie exactly to your tastes without worrying about tight financial schedules. So, if you wish, you can design your film right down to the last detail and re-shoot each scene over and over until you are happy with it. Plan in advance what shots you want to catch on film and what action you want to shoot.

Create a storyboard

When I create my storyboards I just use stick men and women drawn on a piece of paper – you would never believe that I graduated with an Honours Degree in Fine Art. How do you differentiate between a stick man and a woman when they are not wearing any clothes? I just draw stick erections and stick-on breasts.

Storyboards are useful for explaining difficult shots or those that are proving hard to visualize. When you are just starting to use a camera, you may well find it useful to storyboard the whole film.

As a rule, keep your drawings simple. Large film production units will employ special storyboard artists who are trained to be able to interpret the director's vision into sketches. However, you don't need to worry too much about it. Just draw sets of large squares on a few sheets of paper and start to fill out the basic shots you want to include, for example where the action changes from one position to another, or where the sex first begins and how you want it to finish. It is useful for you have idea of where you are going so that you have a visual guide to refer to. It helps enormously having a drawing to point to if you are finding it difficult to explain to your partner what position you want them to get into.

STANDARD PORN SHOTS

If you think of yourself as an aficionado of adult movies, you will probably have noticed that there are some typical shots that appear in virtually every erotic film of the last twenty years. Why is this so? Is it simply that the director lacks imagination or simply can't be bothered to try something new? While that may sometimes be true, it is a fact that there are some standard camera angles that work very well.

The purpose of most porn films is to show all that there is to see. The shots are framed to show as much as possible. You may not like this approach and people often complain that some shots are too 'in your face' (if you'll excuse the expression) leaving nothing to the imagination. One example is the gynaecological shot, that is, a close-up of genitals filling the whole frame. For other people these are their favourite shots. So it is very subjective. Let your instincts drive you, because in the end, the final result is for your enjoyment.

The following are the standard professional shots, but you can use whatever works for you. They are listed under the actions they depict:

Oral sex

Blow job (Fellatio): a man standing and a woman kneeling.

- Objective – a wide-angled shot of the whole situation including the location/setting (see picture 1).
- Close-up side – a head-and-shoulders shot of the woman's head going up and down, showing the man's erection as well (see picture 2).
- Male point of view – a shot taken from above showing what the man sees when he looks down. This works best if the woman is looking up, straight into the camera, and you will need a ladder and a wide angle on your camera. This shot, known as the 'BJ eyes', was first used by porn auteur Michael Ninn in his film *Black Orchid* in the early 1990s. You can include a facial cum shot (the man ejaculating on the woman's face) if you wish.
- Back of head – a medium-wide shot of the action filmed so that the woman's head hides the erection. This shot is usually found in softcore films where the inclusion of an erection is censored (see picture 3).
- Female point of view – this is very rarely shown in conventional films, but I always include it. It is the same as the male point of view, only looking up from the woman's perspective.

Female head (Cunnilingus): a woman sitting in a chair with man kneeling on floor.

- Objective – a wide-angled shot showing the whole situation at once and, to a certain extent, the location/setting.
- Close-up side – a head-and-shoulders shot of the man's head between the woman's legs showing him licking her.
- Male point of view – a shot looking into the woman's spread legs. This can be a close-up gynaecological shot or a medium-wide shot showing her legs in the air, for example.
- Female point of view – a shot over the woman's shoulder looking between her legs. A good shot to try is the female point of view of a woman receiving oral sex while sitting on top of her man, because you can see what he would look like with a beard.

The female point of view

One element of my work that I have always stressed as of the utmost importance for a female viewer to enjoy the scene, is to shoot from her point of view. What I mean by this 'female point of view' is the view a woman has of a scene, whatever act is being portrayed, from her own eyes. Usually in adult movies women have to engage vicariously in a scene from either a neutral or the male perspective. So her enjoyment of the scene is through the male's eyes. This often means if, say, a woman is receiving oral sex from a man in an average erotic movie, the camera shot will not be looking down between her legs at the man as she would see it in real life. The shot is far more likely to be over the man's shoulder towards her. It requires quite a leap of the imagination to make you feel that you can experience what is happening to the woman.

When you make your film, remember there are two of you with two sets of eyes and two points of view possible from any situation, so you should both try using the camera. A woman wants to see her man!

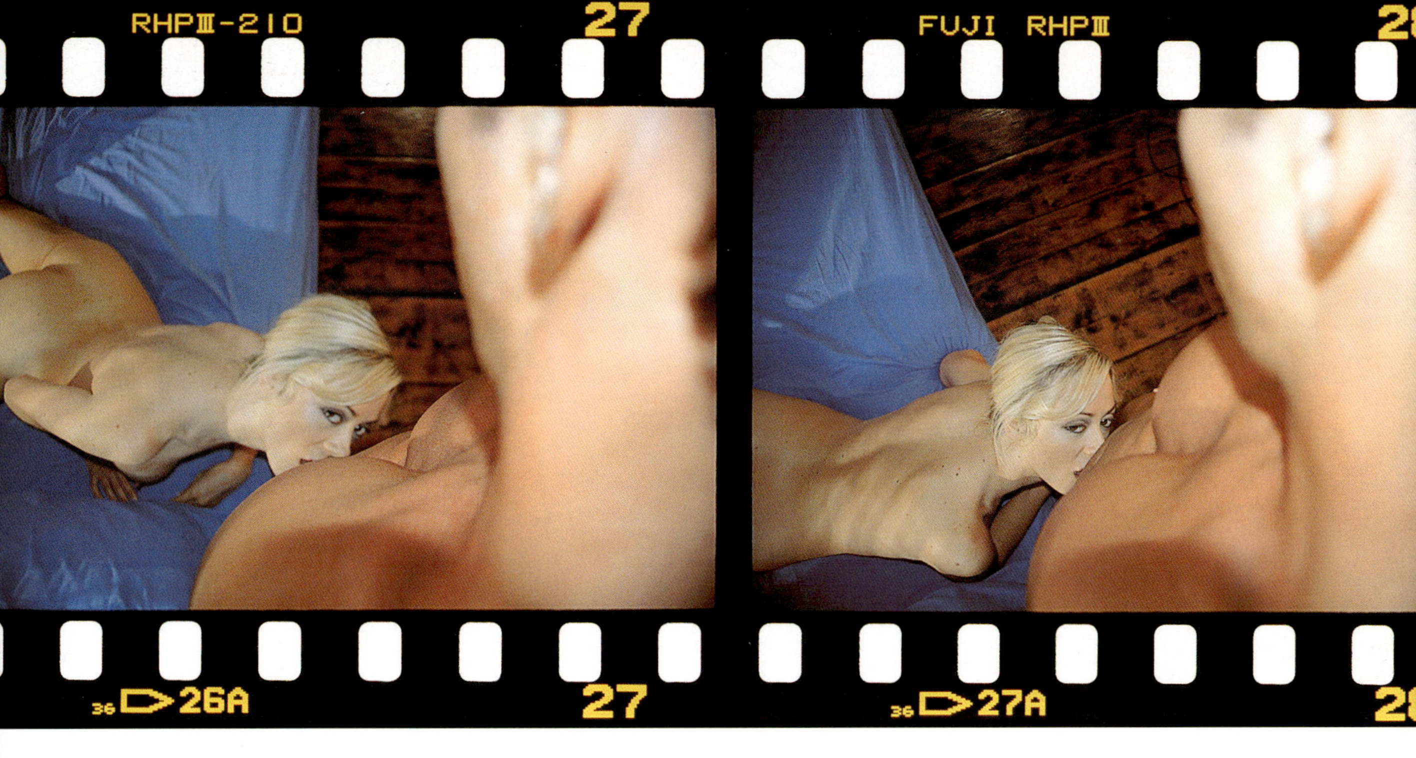

Dildos and toys

If you and your partner want to use dildos and other toys, you can be filmed using the same angles of shot as those in the oral sex section on page 55.

Penetrative sex

The main shots that are normally used include close-up gynaecological shots in which all you can see is the point of penetration; objective shots where you might see most of the participants' bodies while they have sex; and medium-wide shots of the action where you can see both participants at a distance. You should also try to include facial head-and-shoulders shots of each other's expressions. Not only do these shots show the individual while they are in the throws of passion – and we all use our faces differently during sex – but they are very useful as 'cut-aways' if you want to stick various pieces of footage together at the editing stage (see Chapter 8, 'Editing').

It is a tradition in adult movies to give each performer a head-and-shoulders shot of themselves as they orgasm as this is their moment of glory! When we have sex sometimes we are so wrapped up in our own pleasure that we don't visually get to enjoy our partner's expression when they orgasm, so it's an excellent opportunity to get it on film. Also, you may want to include the 'cum shot' or 'money shot' as it is known, when the man actually ejaculates. It's called the money shot because this is the point at which, if the man held out for long enough and ejaculated on the director's cue, he would get paid.

Film your movie from both your own and your partner's perspectives for the best results.

There has been quite a bit of discussion about the predominance of the male 'cum shot' in adult movies. Since women started making pornography in the 1980s, some say that a male orgasm should happen internally, that is, inside the woman. However, it has become a bit more of a regular act for the man to withdraw and ejaculate externally (if you are not using condoms – which you should be!).

When a man ejaculates externally you have 'proof of pleasure' which, according to Linda Williams in her excellent book *Hardcore*, is what the pornography industry has always tried to express with women. It has always been a problem in a genre based on sight and sound, where you see everything so graphically, to have to accept that the female orgasm is naturally internal (with a few exceptions) and therefore will always be a softcore moment.

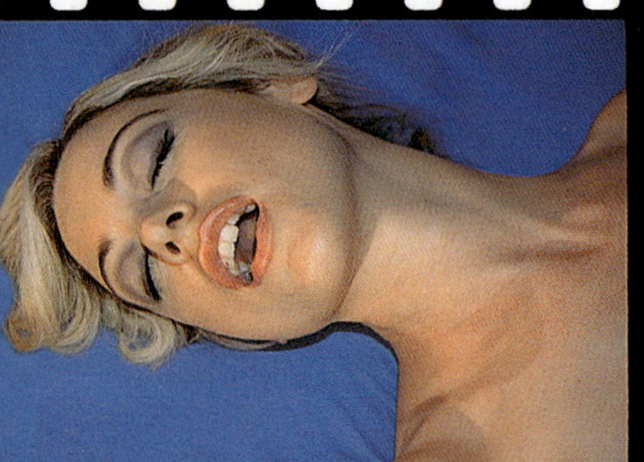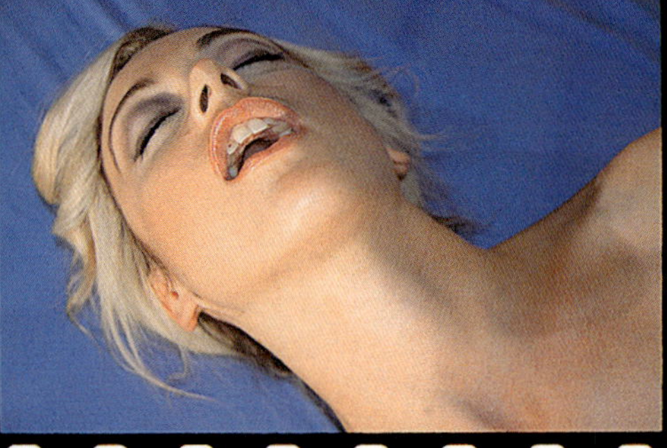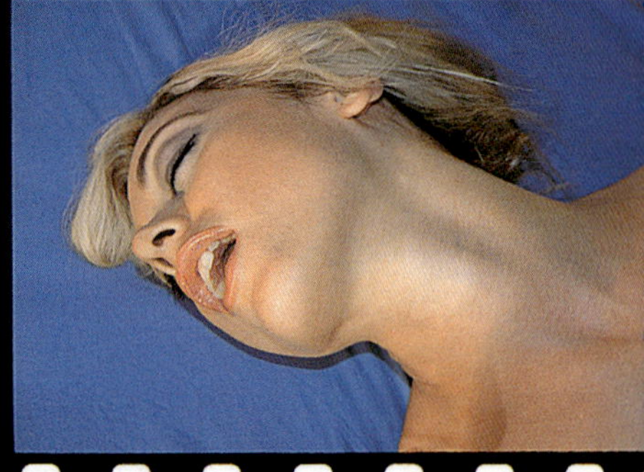

Some women have taken exception to the male 'cum shot' being seen as the main focus of the pleasure in the film. It's up to you as to whether you agree with them or not. Personally, I don't have a problem with external ejaculations although they can look very staged and awkward when you are trying to film sex naturally. I make sure that if the woman needs penetration to reach orgasm I film that first before the man ejaculates, because once he loses his erection, it is less likely that the woman will be completely satisfied.

Watching yourself

You may both want to watch what you are filming as it happens while you are filming. This is possible if your camera has a pull-out LCD viewfinder screen. Also, check to see whether the LCD screen can be flipped over, allowing you to alternate between you and your partner's viewpoint of the same action.

Sometimes when I am filming a scene and I am shooting physically very close to one of the models, I flip the screen so they can see what I am filming of them while I do it. This can be another turn-on.

What's your point of view?

While on the subject of 'points of view', remember that what you shoot will be for both of you to watch, so don't film anything that might cause your partner to get upset with you when it's over and you replay your film. Be sure to include shots of your partner's head and face as well as their body. A continual ten-minute shot of your girlfriend's backside while you penetrate her in the doggie position might not go down too well if you don't occasionally pan up to her head. Equally, it's important that the woman does not let her attention wander and start filming her shoes or chipped nail polish, while her boyfriend is giving her oral sex and trying out a variety of learned strokes of which he is particularly proud. If there is just the two of you, taking it in turns to hold the camera while filming will automatically give you both perspectives.

Hand-held filming

Different ways of using a camera will give to the final film different feels. This is, of course, true of all film, not just erotic movies.

In commercial pornography there are two main types of film: the glossy studio films and the 'Gonzo' or candid type. Apart from lighting (see Chapter 7, 'Lighting and Sound') one of the main differences between the two types of film is that Gonzo is invariably shot using a hand-held camera, rather than the tripod, jib, crane or steadicam-mounted cameras of the glossy studio films.

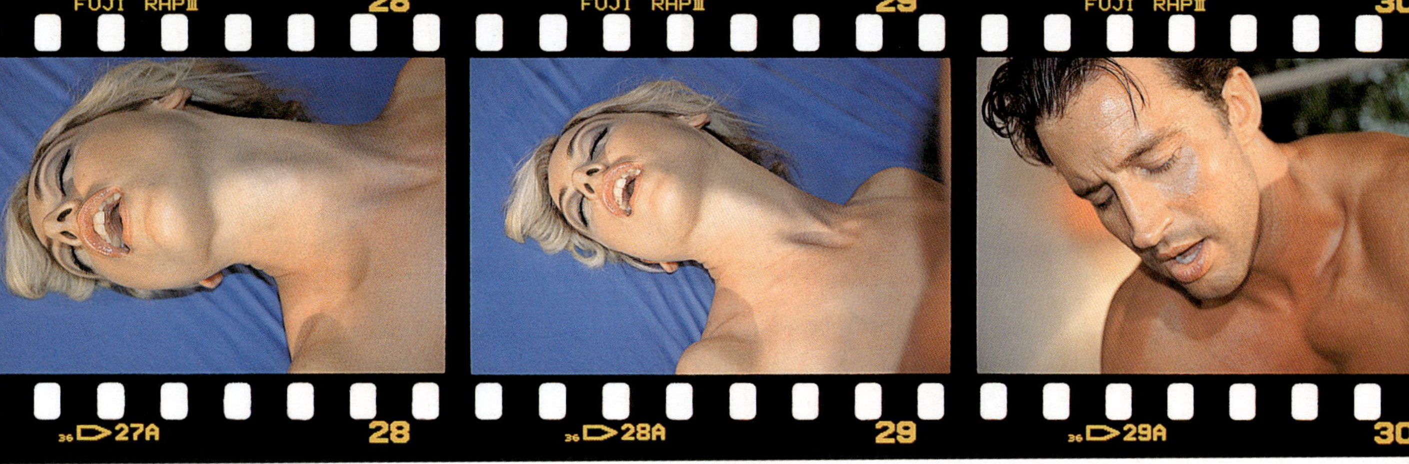

Gonzo films often include the cameraman (it is nearly always a man) as part of the plot. The walking and talking from behind the camera all go to support the idea that this is reality. Restricting the camera to a specific person's point of view has its own dynamic. When you see sex filmed from a camera with a voice behind it and the with realistic movement of the cameraman, you feel more as though you are actually involved; the tripod-mounted, objective camera point of view does not have this effect.

You can use this to your advantage. You can make your film seem very much 'the two of you, in a room, getting down to it on the sofa', without the viewpoint seeming somehow distant. This is especially true if the person behind the camera uses their hands to do things in front of the camera, removing clothes, moving limbs or masturbating their partner, say. For some reason, this is really exciting to see if you fancy the person behind the camera, and really perverse and off-putting if you don't. The mixture of the camera with its traditional perception of power and the furtive human hand is always a winner! Some porn directors build their whole career on the 'one free hand' principle, and the 'film yourself at it with the model in the mirror' shot.

If you do want to use a camera in a hand-held style, remember that a hand-held camera is only as steady as the hand that holds it. Here are some tips on holding a camera steady:

- If you are just filming, as opposed to taking part, hold the camera firmly with both hands and tuck your elbows tightly into your sides. It helps if you put the eyepiece to your eye.
- Assume a stable body position, such as standing evenly balanced with your legs braced.

- Sit down or kneel with each elbow on a knee.
- Lie down on your stomach with a heap of clothes between your elbows and chest to give you support.
- Use something sturdy nearby as a support – lean on a wall or rest against a lamp-post.
- Rest your elbows on a car, low wall, or fence.

The way you use your camera will dictate the feel of the final film.

Different varieties of shot

The glossier types of adult movie tend to use more established cinema film shots. These are not suited to the Gonzo style because they take a lot more time and money, and they are a lot more complicated to set up. What this obviously means is that they require more crew members to change the camera position in between shots. So you automatically need a bigger set. All this effects the timing and flow of the shoot, and is probably not the route you should try initially. You may feel, however, that you want to graduate to it at a later date. The basic shots are shown overleaf.

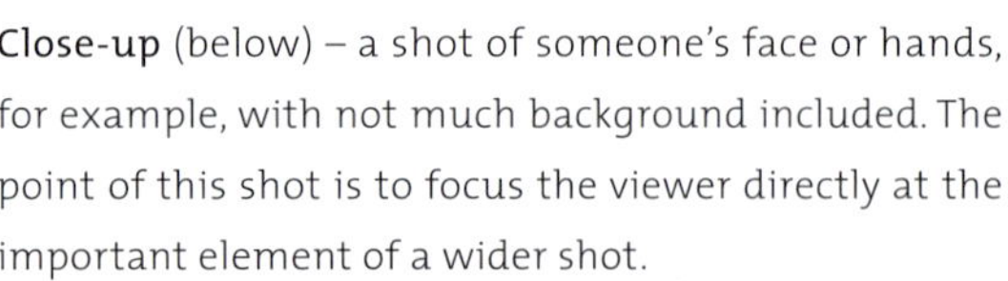

Wide shot (above) – a wide-angled shot used to show
the environment where the action is taking place. This
may, for example, be an aerial view of the house to
establish the location of the story.

Extreme close-up (below) – this is similar to the close-
up, except that its focus is in even more detail: a person's
lips might fill the screen, for example, leaving no room
for anything else. Note that the slightest movement of
your subjects may remove them from the frame.

Medium shot (above) – usually an upper body or head-to-
knee shot that clearly shows the performer and their
surroundings, with the performer as the focal point of the
shot. This offers an uncritical general-purpose viewpoint
from which to watch the action unfold.

Filming tips

- The more you zoom into a scene to get a close-up (bottom left), the more your shot will show camera shake as the smallest movement is magnified. Also, if you are looking through the viewfinder and you zoom in, it is difficult keeping track of the subjects should they move out of the frame. In this case you may then find yourself constantly repositioning the camera to 'catch' your subjects in the frame.

- Scenes shot with a wider angle, say a wide shot or wide-medium shot will, after a while, become boring and frustrate the viewer because they feel the need 'to see more'. Ironically, this means closing in on a scene and focusing on less, that is, by using a close-up. We need to see things in detail as well as placing these details within the context of a scene as a whole. Basically, we want it every way.

Five senses to two rule

As with all film, the human experience is conveyed as a story via the two senses to which cinema can appeal – sight and hearing. The other senses – touch, smell and taste – are not engaged in the experience of the film. And eating popcorn doesn't count!

The same rule applies to erotic movies, but because their purpose is sexually to excite by letting you envisage yourself having sex in the situation on screen, imagining the feelings, smells and tastes associated with sex physically, you have to make quite a leap in the imagination to vicariously enjoy the experience.

Real sex utilizes all five senses together, but on film you only have two senses with which you must portray that excitement. So you must exaggerate the sight and sound in your film to compensate for the three other senses not being present. This is why most adult movies make such prevalent use of exaggerated sex noises and movements – in order to evoke the three missing senses.

- You will notice when you start to shoot the act of sex, that if you do not position yourselves well, you will not be able to see any of the detail of the action. If you are kissing or having sex as you would naturally – the way that gives you the most pleasure – much of the action will be obscured from view. To enable you to see everything, as you do in professional adult movies, you will have to adjust your positioning and be conscious of where the camera is. Position yourself one-third towards the camera (as shown above), revealing a clear view of the point of contact or penetration. You need to do this for all

Position yourselves one-third towards the camera.

positions. You will soon realize that this reduces the physical sensation and the whole thing feels very strange. Being a porn star isn't as easy as you thought!

• It is also important to shoot what are referred to as 'cut-aways'. These are shots used by the editor to edit together two separate shots that would otherwise be impossible to edit together smoothly. To read more about cut-aways see page 119.

PACING

Everybody likes their sex paced differently. Some people like things to be slow and subtle while others like it hard and fast. The same is true for erotic movies. The market today is comprised of many different types of film. One element that differentiates one adult film from another may well be the pace at which the action of the story takes place.

Pace is decided by the way several elements work together: the speed at which the actors perform sex; how long they take to perform in each position; how the director interprets the timing and development of the scene; and how the editor puts together the final story.

Most individual sex scenes in professional erotic films are between ten and 25 minutes long, but you can make the scene as long or short as you wish. You may know how you normally like your sex to be paced, maybe you have already talked about introducing more or less foreplay into your routine, or the man practising holding on for as long as possible before he has an orgasm.

It is important to remember that the pace of your film is not necessarily dictated by the type of sex acts you perform. For example, a slower-paced film need not have a large proportion of foreplay and just a little penetrative sex. Foreplay itself can 'up' the pace of a movie depending on how it is shot. Using film you can convey the passage of time without literally having to show every minute, if that's what you want. So, whereas in real life the foreplay stage often takes longer than that of penetration, you can edit your film so that all your sex acts take the same amount of time. Some adult films do not feature penetrative sex at all, especially S & M and fetish movies.

Film the acts that turn you on

A sensual massage, for example, is great – it can awaken your senses and make every nerve in your body stand to attention, ready for foreplay and penetrative sex. But if you were watching yourself doing exactly the same acts in real time – at the speed it actually happened – you would become bored and start reaching for the fast forward button. Why? The five senses to two rule (see page 61). There is no way on film that you can experience every moment of pleasure, including what you felt, smelt and tasted. Because the two remaining senses of sight and sound are not getting enough stimulus to compensate, you will get bored more quickly.

So you have two options: either you shoot a shorthand version of the massage scene, for example – picking the moves that get the feeling of the whole massage across, or you film 30 minutes of massage and edit it down to just two minutes. However, if you do this, take care not to chop up any live music you might have had playing while you shot the scene. A 30-minute massage can easily be filmed to take up two minutes in the final film, and two minutes will seem like 30 minutes when you come to watch it – I assure you!

When I shoot an erotic movie we can be working all day on just one scene that will eventually be edited down to 20 minutes, so one of the key skills to cultivate is the ability to choose your favourite bits.

It may be the case that one of you would like the film to be slow paced and one of you would like the pace to be much faster. I always try to incorporate both a slow build-up and a fast climax in my films, so maybe you can film both too, to satisfy both of you.

Work to a climax

The same rules of holding a viewer's attention on a mainstream action movie apply to an erotic film and, surprisingly, the challenge is just as great. We tend to work towards a climax even though real sex is not always like that. Some people will say that this is not necessarily the female experience of sex, which consists of more plateaux and waves of sensation, but how good this looks on film is debatable. As I've said, I always film the women coming first and the men coming second, for logistical reasons.

We all like a story with a beginning, a middle and an end, although other experiments of narrative can be very interesting. So, if you want your film to be solely made up of shots of foreplay with no lead-up and no penetrative climax, then I'd advise you to make the foreplay have a beginning, middle and end, in itself. The final result will be much more stimulating. There are few things less stimulating than a scene with no explanation of why you are where you are, and with no fixed route to follow. I have always received fan mail saying that the lead-up and pacing of my work are two of the things fans love about what I do. So decide where you are going before you start.

When I was learning about scriptwriting, my tutor gave an excellent example to illustrate why we need structure in a film. He described a recent night out with an old friend. Instead of organizing a plan for the evening, say cinema, dinner and then drinks, they arranged to meet in a bar and then make the decision of where to go. After a couple of drinks, they went to see what was on at the cinema, but the film they wanted to see had already started. Then they couldn't decide where to eat, so they decided to have another drink. They couldn't agree, so they finally bought a take-away meal. After the take-away the momentum of the evening had gone, so instead of another drink they said goodbye and went home fairly sober and disappointed. Because they had not made a plan, the evening had no trajectory and eventually the participants lost interest. The same is true of film.

In professional pornography there are certain timings for scenes that are considered to be the norm. I find that having a five to six minute build-up, followed by seven to eight minutes of foreplay, and then a similar amount of time for penetrative sex, is a formula that works well for most of my viewers.

You can film the breaks in between sexual positions as well, as these can act as a refresher stage – both while you are making the movie and while you are watching it – before moving on. When you start having sex again you can be much more vigorous than when you started in the previous position. But don't add too many scenes of you and your partner in different positions, or your film could start to look like a string of positions without ever really developing to any particular end. This can be very frustrating to watch because you need to feel that the scene is going in one definite direction, just as you do when you are actually having sex – if you are pumping away and don't feel that the sexual energy is building you can lose the momentum to continue.

Actual sex should hopefully take longer than would its portrayal in an adult movie. Mainstream narrative cinema works on the same principle so that most films lasting around one and three-quarter hours are nearly always telling a story that took place over hours, days, weeks or even years.

Ultimately, the pacing of your film will be down to you, and as long as you have enough footage you can always make changes when you get to the editing stage of your movie. Gradually you will improve your movie-making technique, and then I'll have to watch out!

When I was a teenager, I was taken to my parents' friends for dinner. When we had eaten the friends asked us if we would like to see their holiday film taken in some distant country. I felt like leaving but wouldn't have got away with it. As I sat and watched one continuous shaky hand-held shot of a bubbling brown mud bath for over 25 minutes, I can remember looking at these friends and thinking 'I can't believe that these people aren't bored yet'. But they weren't. They sat smiling at their work, completely contented, and seeing it in a completely different way to how I was. It just goes to show that pace and content ultimately are a matter of taste.

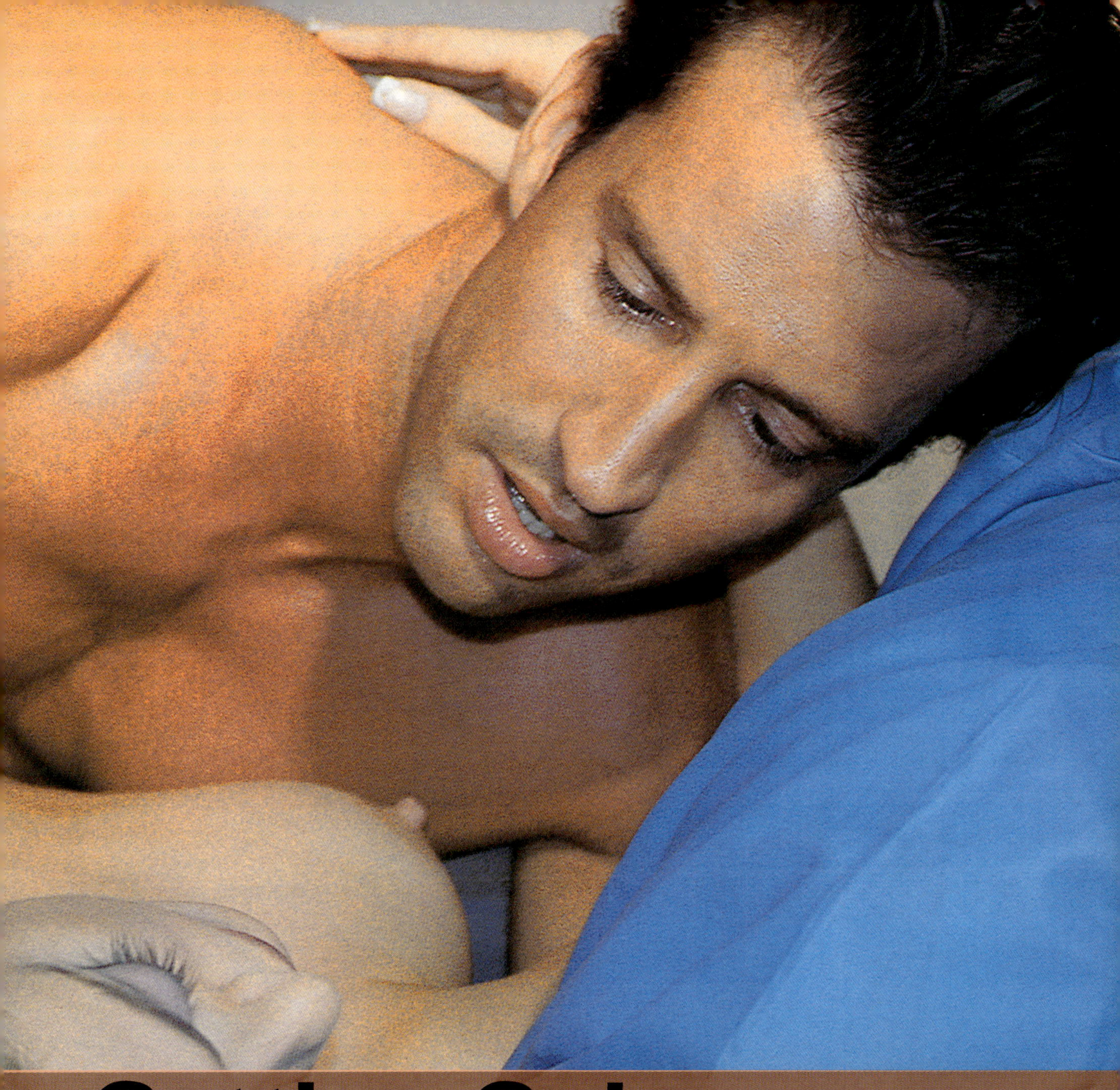

Getting Going

You've got your costumes and camera, you've done your make-up, he's got his comedy moustache on, you're clutching your storyboard, and you've dispatched the kids to stay the night with their grandparents... What now? Well, now it's time to take the leap into porno world!

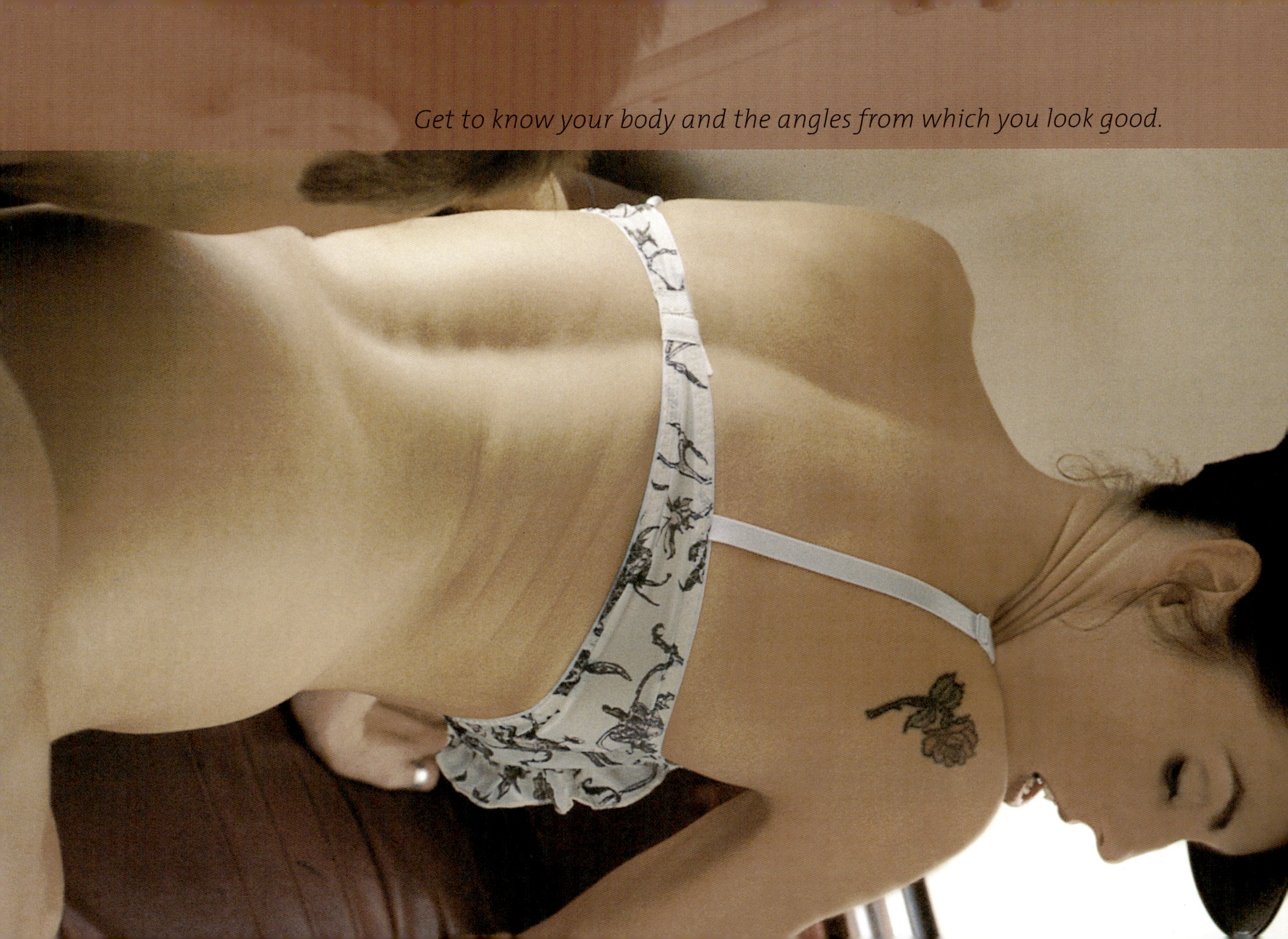
Get to know your body and the angles from which you look good.

Getting Going

The only thing you need to remember about the whole experience is to have fun and let yourselves go. Remember that you have many opportunities available to you and a lot of time on your hands. If you like making this film, which I'm sure you will, you can always go on to try other variations on the erotic theme until you create a repertoire that really gets you going. Explore different scenarios, positions, props and acts in order to find the ones that really hit the spot. And remember, practise makes perfect. So, stop thinking about doing it and working towards doing it, and start doing it.

For most people the idea of being filmed having sex will stir up mixed feelings. On the one hand, there is the excitement of trying something new, especially as it is considered to be quite naughty. On the other hand, all of this might only seem like a good idea if you can guarantee that you will look good and perform amazingly. After all, I doubt that if you have ever dreamed of being a porn star that you envisaged yourself as a bad one. If you've watched adult movies and said 'I could do better than that', you may well be right. But just before you actually get down to it, it is natural to experience some anxiety about your physical appearance or your performance.

In this chapter I offer some advice and tips on getting over some of the psychological and physical hurdles that you might experience.

DEALING WITH NERVES

So what do you do? Well, there are several ways you can help yourself and/or your partner to relax. The first option is to talk about it. It's alright to admit to being nervous if you haven't tried something like this before, and the chat doesn't have to be a deep, hand-wringing discussion. After all, it's your film, and it's just for you to watch.

The next thing to consider is what it is that is making you nervous. Maybe a general feeling of unease can be dissipated if you are specific. You may discover that it is starting off the film with the camera on you that is making you nervous. So maybe a way around this is for you to start with the camera in your hands, focusing on your partner (assuming they're not nervous as well). Or maybe you

Sometimes nerves can help your final performance.

Although I love to strip for my partner, it is another thing entirely to strip in front of a camera – in a strange way, it feels like there is a huge audience present.

One way to help alleviate this apparent attention is for the person behind the camera to give directions and specific instructions to the stripper as to what to take off next. Of course, if any positive comments about your partner occur to you at this stage, it will help to actually voice the complement.

In general, I think having a positive attitude towards the times when you are less confident can really help. It's natural sometimes to get nervous just before something new, and it helps if you view these times as opportunities to extend your confidence and repertoire. Areas that cause the most anxiety beforehand are nearly always the ones that give the greatest reward once you have achieved them. Trying new things regularly will also keep you fresh-minded and able to spot other opportunities.

Ask your partner to direct you as you strip. are about to perform an act that you are not normally very confident about. In this case I suggest that you start with another one, or go back to one you have already performed successfully.

Stripping

One act that prompts considerable nerves in some performers is stripping. Now this I can understand.

It's a flop

As a professional adult film director, I deal with porn stars' nerves every day. Although both the men and the women that I film often suffer from nerves, it's that bit more obvious when the men are lacking confidence, if you know what I mean. In this situation, it is very important to be sensitive; it is a very demanding job and not many men are able do it as a profession.

If you are having problems with nerves and your man can't achieve an erection, I suggest you turn the camera off for a while and get down to it without thinking about filming. Just remember to turn it back on again when you are ready to go!

The good thing about shooting a home movie is that you have no time limits. It's not as though you have to finish the film by a specific date. As long as you keep

an eye on continuity (see page 123) and make sure the location and your clothes are the same, you can come back another day and finish off the scene. I think it is essential that you really believe that making this erotic movie is as important as the end product. So just have fun.

On film your natural sex positions may look clumsy.

PERFORMANCE TIPS

So you want me to make you a porn star in your own bedroom? Well, I can give you some tips to help you polish your existing talents in order that your performance is worthy of a pro, and there are also some hints and ideas I can give you as to what positions to try, but I'm afraid I can't work miracles and make you perform like a Brazilian god or goddess. You just have to be honest with your partner and simply communicate about what you both like and dislike.

Exaggerate your moves

Erotic movies are like Bollywood. Bollywood is regarded as a form of cinema based on a particular style of acting, that is the externalized expression of inner desires and feelings. The performers 'act out physically' the feeling they are experiencing in a very clear story-telling style. There can be no misunderstanding of what the character is saying.

Erotic movies also sing their sensations out loud. No need to reach for your Stanislavski handbook on the 'Method' approach to acting to establish whether the stars are enjoying themselves.

It is all a matter of technique. Remember the 'five senses to two' rule, which means you only have sight and sound to utilize in order to depict the experience. So you have to perform in such a way as to make the most of the two senses you do have at your disposal. And their stimulus needs to be exaggerated.

A naturally satisfying position may not make the best position for an erotic movie. The missionary position, if performed in the usual manner, will resemble two sacks of potatoes come viewing time. You will be shocked at how inactive you both look (see above left). This is because when it comes to seeing sex on tape, the porn industry

Create space between your bodies so that your shape and features can be seen by the camera.

has it pretty well worked out as to which elements work and which don't.

Exaggerated movement is one such element. When you are having sex for film you need to exaggerate every movement to hold your viewers' attention on it (and therefore the resulting physical sensation) when it comes to show time. So if you are a man performing penetration doggie style, you want to slide your erection in deeper and out further than you would normally. And remember to keep your hips one-third facing the camera. Bringing the erection further out not only enhances the movement, but also makes your manhood look longer, because if you pull back to just

before the head appears, on film your erection could still have a length inside the woman. But beware! As I am sure you are already aware through your own sex life, full inward and outward movement results in air being pumped into the woman which, although it feels great for her at the time, can also cause cramps and certain less-than-erotic noises afterwards.

Use your hands and mouth

Also, when you are performing, try to tell a story with your hands and tongue. They are very good at making you think of how the body you are touching feels or tastes. Slow down and use your hands in a definite way.

Let them caress the skin as if they have a will of their own and you will engage with the feeling again when you watch it later. The tongue is great for expressing sexual hunger and the teasing of the flesh. It is also very good for defining the shape of the body that you are touching. Your head and tongue will move up and down and all around when you lick your partner's contours, especially areas like the small of the back and behind the knee. Slowing down this hand and tongue movement seems to exaggerate it, especially when the contact is soft, barely touching at all. This works well when shot in close-up.

They say that if you want to exaggerate something in the cinema, you should use a little of the opposite to highlight it. For example, you can have a room that is completely silent but you won't notice it until you drop a pin and hear the sound it makes. Then suddenly you become very aware of the silence, before and after the act. Feeling the touch of a feather or finger on the skin produces a similar effect. This light touch brings your attention to the previous lack of touch and the following lack of touch, thus exaggerating the feel of the feather.

Think of the camera

In erotic movies, all sexual positions are supported by one or other of the models, so they don't both resemble a sack of potatoes. In the missionary position, the man always supports himself and pushes backwards slightly, away from the woman, so the camera can get close up to see everything. The man is also careful not to obstruct the shot with a limb, even though his natural impulse is to position it in a totally different place. This results in the position common in adult films: the man is standing, pumping away with his hand on the small of his back.

If the woman is on top, she automatically stretches out lengthwise and holds that position for the whole scene in order for the camera to see her fully. She might naturally grab onto her partner's shoulders to give

herself leverage, but this would mean that her arms would be obstructing the action.

Look at the lens

I'm constantly amazed when I see films in which the performers seem to have an aversion to looking at each other (see bottom left). Use your eyes, either to look at the camera or at each other, and be aware of where your face is in relation to the camera. When you come to watch the film you will see that looking at the camera is very erotic.

It is very daring to look straight into the camera lens. It translates as 'I know you are looking' and either 'I don't

care' or 'I like it.' Edouard Manet used this in his famous painting *Le Déjeuner sur l'Herbe* (1863), in which a naked woman, sitting among a group of smartly dressed men, stares smiling straight into the viewer's eye, as if to say 'Do you like what you see?' The painting caused a furore in the art establishment, and it was rejected from the famous Paris Salon. Manet had been very successful until then and so started a new salon, 'La Salon Des Réfusés', which only showed work that had been rejected as 'bad art' by the establishment. *Et voila*! Modern art was born.

Look at the camera during sex, not into the corners of the room.

Genuine facial expressions and graphic camera angles are extremely erotic.

A person's face can say a lot, especially if the eyes are genuinely dilated from desire. But be careful not to overdo it. The difference between a genuine expression of desire or sexual satisfaction and the countenance of a grimacing lunatic is only a matter of degree.

Your best angles

Get to know your body and the angles from which you look good. Many of you are already aware of what is your best side from seeing photos of yourself. Now you should really look at yourself in the nude. If you have a large stomach, try out positions which make it look less 'obtrusive'. Avoid low-level camera angles, which will exaggerate your stomach if you are looking up at it.

Sagging breasts look better on film if you wear a bra that lets you pull them out of the top – then they will look good in almost any position. Doggie style especially, if filmed from the front without a bra, will make sagging breasts look bad. This position makes many breasts, even quite firm ones, look thinner, although small breasts that also hang will look bigger in this position.

The only really flattering position if your breasts sag is on your back because they stand up more, and although they do fall towards your armpits, this is still an improvement on hanging breasts. You can also turn slightly to one side while on your back with only one shoulder touching the bed, so that one of your breasts sticks out on top, at the opposite angle to your hips. This position is good for a nipple-sucking shot.

Anything that you position at an upside-down angle will be subject to gravity and shooting from underneath is very unflattering unless you are very well toned. Gravity is exaggerated even more when you add movement. A sagging breast looks bad enough from underneath; a swinging sagging breast is twice as bad. So you will have to try to keep a certain poised position throughout the film.

Porn posture

Keeping a conscious eye on your posture will help a lot. To assist you in this, imagine a taut string attached to the top of your head pulling your body so that it is taller in all positions.

Another way to make your posture more 'racehorse-like' is to curve the back slightly, which has the added advantage of pushing out the chest and backside. A curved back looks amazing on a woman in most positions but especially the cowgirl or doggie position, as it accentuates the curves and the difference of size between your shoulders and your hips, making the waist look even smaller.

But beware! Banging away in this position for any length of time can give you quite bad backache because you are causing the force of the movement to be concentrated on the small of the back rather than allowing it to dissipate through the whole of the upper body. So my advice is to use the curved back position sparingly and to make sure that when you do use it, you get it on film.

> Having played the part of a prostitute/erotic dancer for a whole afternoon during my A-level Theatre Studies course, in which I was proudly showing off my back-bending skills, later I reached down to get a pint of milk from the bottom of the refrigerator and my back completely locked. I couldn't even return to the standing position, let alone walk. So I just had to hang in there, upside down, until someone came to help. And refrigerators are cold, mean places.

The legs of most men look just as good, or bad, on film as they do in real life, but women are often prone to cellulite and are rarely keen to be reminded of it, especially in their own erotic movie. So what do you do? Well, there are definite ways to improve the textures of your skin on screen. The golden rule is not to light upwards! Instead, you should angle the light so that it is straight on, parallel to the cellulite. In this way each little 'crater' – if you think of it in terms of being like the surface of the moon – is filled with light and doesn't cast any shadows.

Keep an eye out for lines on the skin left by underwear. The underwear doesn't have to be too tight to leave a mark, although it is definitely worse if it is. To avoid this, only wear the underwear for as short a time as possible beforehand, or leave time for the marks to fade naturally between taking off your clothes and shooting the scene. Of course, the other alternative is not to wear any underwear at all. One last thing: men, do remember to take your socks off – especially the English.

POSITIONS

There are hundreds of positions that have been thought of to spice up the human act of reproduction. You can do it every which way you like. Just the slight change in the angle of a limb and you've discovered a new position with a new name. It seems that some people's thirst to try out and name new-found positions knows no bounds. To complicate matters, there seems to be no consensus on what to call positions, and each position probably has four or five names. So it's possible that you could find yourself in a situation that ends up, despite having agreed a position with your partner, with you head-butting each other as you move in opposite directions. I won't try to name them all, but I will give a brief outline of the main positions to try, giving their professional porn-industry name where it's appropriate.

It's worth remembering that a woman has as many sexually sensitive areas inside her as outside. You can see, and hopefully find, the outer areas – the clitoris and inner and outer labia, say – but the G-spot and A-spot are harder to locate. Some positions allow you to hit these spots without even trying. So, here is a quick introduction to female sexual anatomy:

The G-spot

Named after Dr Grafenberg, the German doctor who 'discovered' it, the G-spot is positioned about 5 cm (2 in) inside the front wall of the vagina. It feels like a spongy area about the size of a coat button and is made up of ridges. It takes some effort to find it and, in fact, some women are not that sensitive there. For a woman, the G-spot is usually where you can feel a warm, pulsating feeling when you are turned on. Sometimes it can feel as though it is internally linked to the clitoris.

The A-spot

The anterior formex erogenous zone, or A-spot for short, has recently been discovered – by the male experts that is – as being situated near the top of the front wall of the vagina. It is where a woman feels the end of the erection/dildo, especially if the couple are in the doggie or spoons position.

Try out different positions to see which make the most of your physique.

The clitoris

The external erogenous bump at the top end of the vaginal opening. If the clitoris is stimulated directly, the sensation it creates can be almost too much; for some women nearby stimulation is preferable.

Labia

The vaginal lips, both outer and inner (pink) are very sensitive. You can stimulate them by rubbing the inside of the outer labia against the inner labia in a flat hand movement. It is also very pleasurable when the whole area is licked. Men often forget the lips when giving oral sex – don't! If the outer lips are shaved, the skin becomes more sensitive, giving the woman an increased sensation. You don't have to shave everything off, just the underside.

The PC muscle

It is useful for both men and women to be aware of their pubococcygeus (PC) or pelvic floor muscle. Exercising this muscle helps the man to maintain control; for the woman it helps with grip and sensation during sex. Pelvic floor exercises also help to keep the bladder and urethra healthy, especially after giving birth.

Pelvic floor exercise

In the 1950s Dr Kegel developed an exercise to help strengthen the PC muscle. So try this. When you next go for a pee try to stop the flow midway. The muscle you are using is your pelvic floor muscle. You need to clench and relax this muscle 20 times in fast succession. Try doing this as many times during the day as you can or as often as you can remember to do it (not just on the toilet). Then try doing a longer clench, holding it in for six seconds at a time. Breathe in when contracting the muscle and exhale when relaxing, bearing down slightly. Keep doing this for about five minutes, if you can stand it. You can do these exercises anywhere as no one will notice – unless, that is, you are screwing up your face without thinking.

Positions for couples

You can shoot sex in any position you like, but some positions, such as spoons, cause problems – obscuring the point of penetration from the camera. The positions below are popular choices for movies because you can film them easily, seeing everything you want as long as you remember to use the 'one-third to camera' rule (see page 61). The positions you will see most frequently in adult movies are:

- Missionary
- Doggie
- Cowgirl (woman on top)
- Reverse Cowgirl (woman on top facing away from man)
- Anal (missionary)
- Anal (doggie style)
- 69
- Oral (lying down)
- Oral (standing up)
- Rimming (oral sex on the anus)

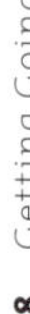

Watching someone masturbate is one of the most exciting experiences possible.

Solo

Another type of erotic genre which involves a couple, but in which you only see one person, is the 'solo' masturbation film. It is still one of the most under-explored sexual acts and, for me, one of the most exciting. To watch someone giving themselves real sexual pleasure, showing them as masters of their own body, is a turn-on for both men and women.

There are many scenes in professional pornography that include shots of a woman touching herself, but few men realize how, for many women, the same act performed by a man is just as likely to be a huge turn-on. If you haven't tried it before, start to masturbate in front of your woman and see how she reacts. Obviously, you need to be aware of your timing. It would be best to start masturbating when you are both in bed, as you begin to get down to sex, rather than standing in front of the television, say, trying to catch her eye as she watches her favourite show.

To this day, masturbation still has a stigma attached to it – for men and women. I think a lot of people still feel guilty about doing it, some so much so that they refrain from it altogether. This is a shame, because it is such a natural thing to do, and doing it in front of your partner in a safe environment, away from prying eyes, can be really sexy. So give it a go.

I actually interview wannabe male porn stars by watching them masturbate without any visual stimulation at all, just the power of speech. Although I do this to test their suitability for the profession, there is nothing to stop you and your partner trying it for recreational purposes. When I have shown these interviews to female friends they have become quite hot under the collar (so much so that I have bought the rights and put them all onto one video for general release).

Fingering on film

Sit your partner opposite you in a hard-backed chair and start asking them questions. You could act out a session of questioning at a police station perhaps, or a more intense interrogation scenario. But I wouldn't go as far as tying their arms behind their backs, because this could prove taxing if you want to see them masturbate.

Start by asking you partner at what age he lost his virginity and what the experience was like. Did he enjoy it? Was it embarrassing? It's fun to talk about when you were both fumbling adolescents, and the embarrassing or funny times you've had in the past. Then ask him how he likes to be touched, which parts of his body are the most sensitive. You may find out that it's somewhere you have never even thought of touching. It happens to us all – think about it as a learning experience! Positive, open-ended questions work well in this situation. It's worth remembering at this point that if the chances are that you will not like the answers to certain questions, you'd do better not to ask those questions. If you are a jealous lover, you should avoid talking about ex-partners and concentrate on asking questions about how he likes you. After all, this isn't meant to be a real inquisition.

you in a very impersonal way, almost as though you are just a body he wants to satisfy sexually. The way you do it is up to you. Choose the tone that turns you on, whether it is personal and supportive or impersonal and matter of fact.

Enjoy his body

Use the camera to look at every aspect of his body. Focus on the parts that you like; tell him you like them; and tell him what part of his body you are looking at. Remember a zoom action on a camera works as a magnifying glass, making far-away objects appear nearer.

Slow down when you are panning over your favourite parts of his body, such as his neck, his shoulders, the back of his knees – or his erection. Ask him to strip a little at a time. Ask him to show you the part you want to see most – maybe he has to turn around or stand up. Remember to tell him what parts are your favourites – don't assume that he knows. We can spend our whole lives not seeing a lot of our own body, such as the back of the knees or the curve of our backside. It's nice to hear that someone has been noticing something beautiful about you of which you are completely unaware.

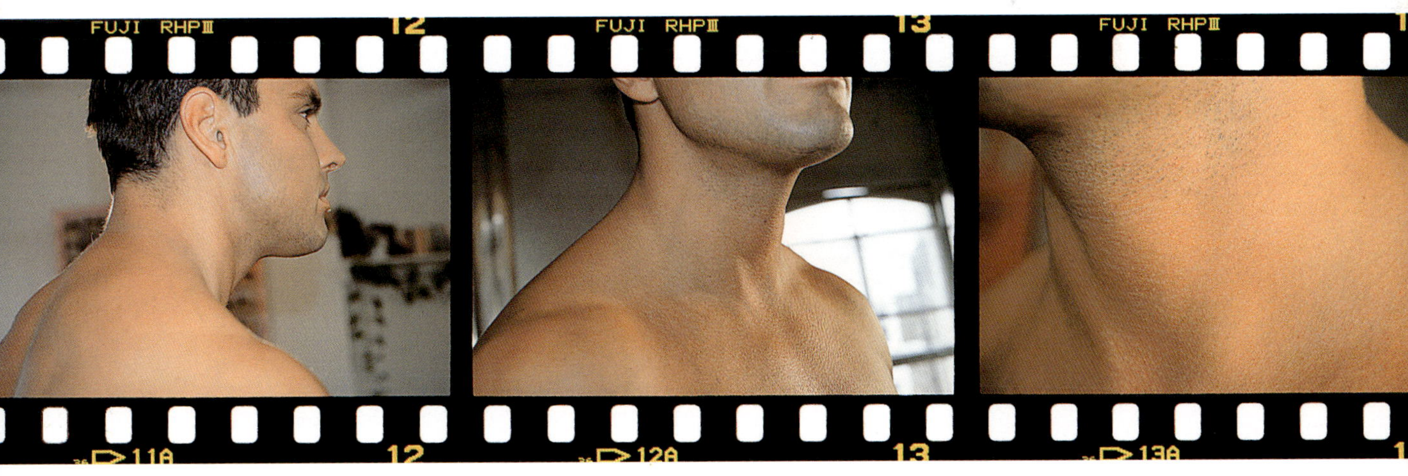

Next ask him to describe in detail his current girlfriend (you, with any luck), saying why he likes her. It can be really sexy if you and your partner talk about each other in the third person, as if you are talking about somebody else. Ask him what he would like to do to this girl, given half the chance. It might excite you if he speaks about

The man can tease you, taking his time to reveal himself. He may refuse at first, so that maybe you have to use some persuasive skills to get him to do as you wish, reprimanding him, for instance, for being disobedient. Another alternative is to position the camera beside you, pointing

Film the areas of your partner's body that you find especially sexy.

at your man, so that you can film him as he watches you strip, without filming your own performance. Maybe you can play the role of peep-show customer and stripper. Watching your man as he gets turned on by looking at you slowly undressing and touching yourself is really provocative. Show him afterwards how sexy he looks when he is not conscious of himself anymore. However conscious of the camera you are when you begin, you can 'lose yourself' in the situation eventually.

Then, when you have tried it one way, you can reverse the roles next time – and get your own back!

You can incorporate the masturbation footage in to film of your partner stripping. Shoot both acts from beginning to end, and at the editing stage, intercut the strip with you masturbating to it, so that you have two separate solo performances. If you want to do this, bear in mind that you should film both performances in the same positions. So, if you are sitting down on a particular corner of the bed facing in a particular direction in the first film, then you need to film your partner stripping from that perspective in the second film, and vice versa.

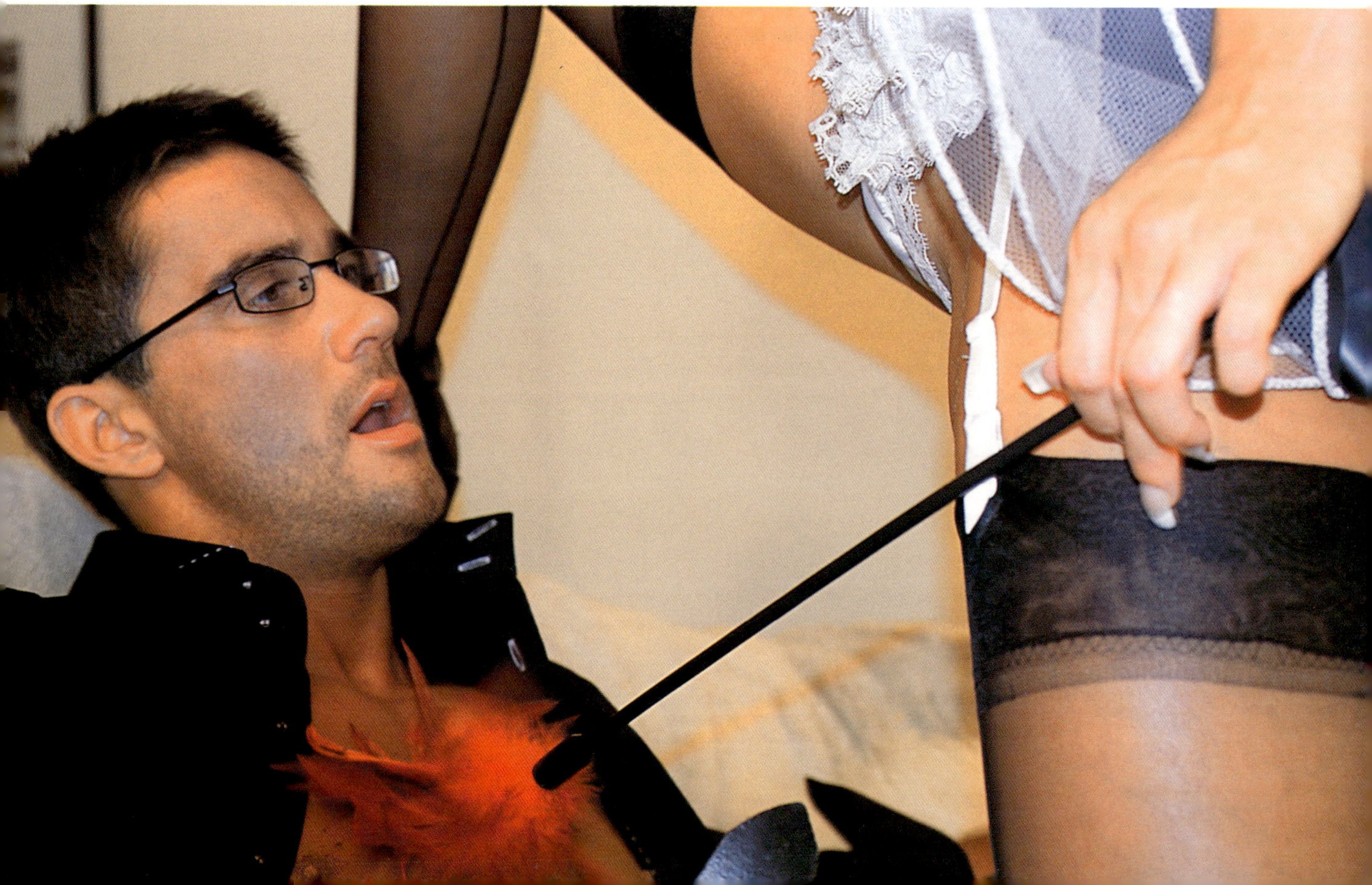

Watching someone perform a personalized strip is very sexy, if you are both willing, especially if you are instructing them as to how exactly you'd like them to do it. Talking from behind the camera while a strip is performed is very naughty because it gives a strong feeling of a professional situation, such as in a lap-dancing club or peepshow. The sight of stuffing money in a garter is also sexy, and there is something innately shocking about the look of flesh next to hard cash that heightens the experience. It says 'My body is for sale, but only to you.' Alas, for the parsimonious of you, I'm afraid toy money just doesn't have the same effect.

Threesomes

If you are lucky enough to know two people who want to sleep with you, maybe you can persuade them to do it simultaneously and maybe even get it on film. If this is the case, are some options that are not possible with just two people in the room suddenly become possibilities. By adding another person to the situation you are increasing the possibilities by a third. Some of the possibilities are:

- Spit roast – one man penetrating the woman while she performs oral sex on someone else.
- Double penetration – one erection is inserted into the vagina and the other into the anus.
- Double penetration – two penises in the same orifice.
- Double oral – one woman performs oral sex on two men simultaneously and vice versa.
- Daisy chain – three or more women giving oral sex or using dildos on each other, in a circle.

From a film-making point of view, the real freedom comes from the fact that you are now able to pass the camera around, which allows you to see the same action from at least two different perspectives. The same action filmed by two different people will show you just how differently they perceive the same act, and also how different you look from your head to your backside! From an editing point of view it allows you to make several shots simultaneously, which you will then be able to edit together as a continuous piece, providing several possibilities at the editing stage (see Editing, page 119).

Bear in mind that threesomes can as easily comprise two men and one woman, as two women and one man. I find that men sometimes forget this.

Group sex

Back in the 1970s they used to call it 'wife swapping'; now they call it 'swinging'. The swinging scene is alive and kicking; there *Close-up shots, including masturbation scenes, reveal the intimate you.* are all sorts of organized orgies happening all over the country – and they are completely legal. If you and your partner (you need a partner – it's a prerequisite for most groups) haven't tried the swinging scene, then you can definitely find out all about it on the Internet, including whether your local area has any groups. There are countless sites on the web that will furnish you with all the relevant details if you search for 'swinging sex' and type in your region.

However, not everyone in a relationship wants to try other partners, even if they do admit to being a bit bored of the sex in their current situation – and that is never a good reason to think about swinging. It is extremely sad when you see that one partner has been talked into participating in group sex because their partner wants an excuse to sleep with other people guilt-free.

There are many groups that specialize in sexual activities, such as sadomasochism and other fetishes. You have to pick wisely or you risk ending up in a room full of excited people who are looking for something from you that is not at all what you're expecting or what you want.

I remember once going to an S & M ball and seeing an amazing game of badminton. There was a court drawn out on the floor and at each end was a man dressed in a school tracksuit and sports shirt, holding an old-fashioned badminton racquet. However, the shuttlecock was a tiny Japanese woman dressed in a white tutu. When the whistle blew the men took it in turns to smack the woman on the bottom with their racquets, sending her running and jumping over the net. When she got to the other 'player' she would bend over ready for a return shot. We all cheered the game on and the poor woman finished up quite out of breath.

Thinking from an erotic movie-making perspective, the swinging scene provides a lot of opportunities as well as a few complications, especially if some of the participants don't want to be filmed. It has to be something that you all agree to.

People are naturally more concerned when you start recording them. They will often be much more liberated in their behaviour if they think that it only exists in the memories of the people present. That indelible videotape might just make them think twice. It seems that to be sexually free is one thing, but to be recorded in full swing is another thing entirely.

However, some people positively thrive under the camera's gaze. Having a camera present can justify stupid or carefree behaviour that the person in question might otherwise perhaps feel less inclined to express – so it works both ways.

Here are some tips you might find useful when you get to filming the orgy:

- Pass the camera around and see how people use it differently. Make sure that the women in the group get a fair turn. It's quite easy to slip into thinking that you use the camera objectively without showing your personality, but different people will do things that surprise you. They may shoot everything in extreme close-up, or maybe one person only wants to film backsides. You can learn a great deal about a person from the way they use a video camera.
- Take turns to direct each other, to tell others what to do, describing exactly how you want them to behave (right down to how loud they moan or what angle to put their leg). It's a nice feeling, being in control of two people having sex (I should know!), but you must do it respectfully. This could be the closest you come to a professional porn-directing situation.
- You can try writing a script if you can get organized. Incorporate all the characters that people want to be, including costumes – although your living room will probably resemble the home of the Village People. The chances are that you can make up a scene off the cuff from any two or more of the characters present, working in their chosen personalities.

You could also add a comic twist to your swinging party. For example, you could film a couple in the missionary position, standing with the camera pointing down at the woman, so that you can see one man pumping away, and then you could zoom in to a close-up of her face in ecstasy. Then you swap the man for another man. If the woman keeps a straight face, or at least the same contorted expression, it would be quite amusing to zoom back out again and see the new man pumping away at the same pace. Just a thought!

Everybody could be in one story, a gangster film, say, with good guys and bad guys. This way, you only need to wear a suit or a dress, and there are enough opportunities for everyone to get to be their type of

character, whether it is a submissive, a harlot, or a stud – you just change the script to fit everyone.

Remember to invite the group to watch the film when you next have a party. It's horny to see yourselves on the TV in the background. It's also interesting to see how people's performances alter when they change partners, or to notice how they don't change at all. The next time you meet up you can use the film as something to whet your appetites, or to break the ice, as I am sure there will be some comic clips, however much you tried to avoid them.

Another place to enjoy group sex is at one of the growing number of sex clubs opening up everywhere. This is especially fun if you are at all into exhibitionism, as you will no doubt attract quite an audience if you start getting down to it straight away. Filming in these establishments is strictly forbidden, however.

GIRL/GIRL AND BOY/BOY

So far, this book has been written with the assumption that you are a heterosexual couple. Descriptions are simply easier that way, but I feel that a lot of what is useful for a heterosexual couple will be equally helpful for a homosexual pair. However, there are definitely some areas to consider more specifically for homosexual couples, for instance, what they may want to try out. Having said that, there may be some things here that a heterosexual couple might want to experiment with.

Girl/Girl

The heterosexual adult film industry has been used to two-girl sex scenes, or 'Girl/Girl' as they are known, for many years. They have been very popular since the late 1970s, although there are examples of lesbian imagery dating back to the invention of photography.

I am naturally interested in filming both men and women, and half my work revolves around girl/girl scenes. I enjoy shooting these scenes and they are easier

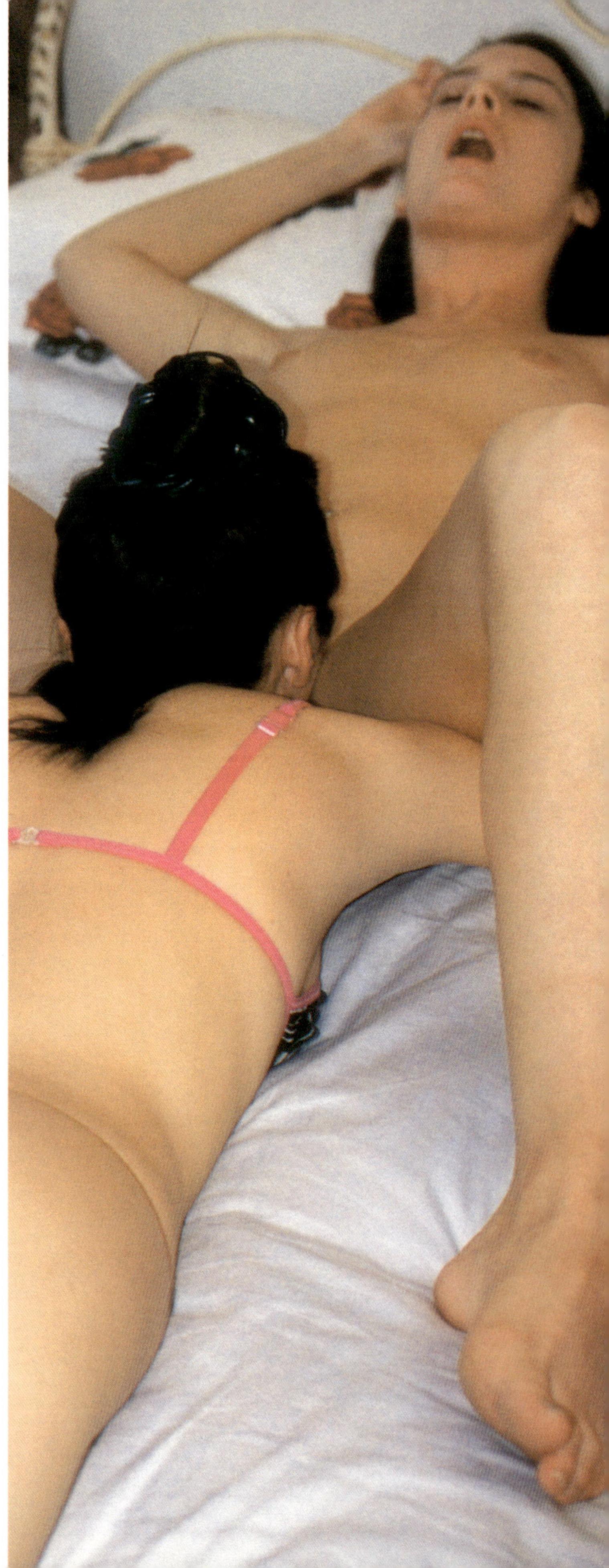

from a professional point of view, because you don't have the legal and logistical implications of filming a man with an erection.

One element of my films that many women apparently enjoy is the emphasis I place on the personality of the characters and their sense of humour. My idea of femininity is also more realistic than a man's; he doesn't have the female experience upon which to draw. Some women complain about all the fake nails and unconvincing orgasms depicted in mainstream lipstick lesbian movies. Unfortunately, there aren't many genuine lesbian productions out there – not compared to the male homosexual market. So you need to make your own!

If you are lesbian, then you will probably want to see much more foreplay than is typically shown in each scene. You may want to see more mutual masturbation as well. Sad though it is, the fingers seem to have been lost to the heterosexual market.

Take plenty of time to explore all your erogenous zones on tape. Whatever it is that you like in real life, you can film to be just as sexually stimulating. But make sure you consider pace: give your scene a beginning, a middle and an end, even if you want to focus solely on one or two acts, such as oral sex.

Boy/Boy

Not only gay men but heterosexual women as well find the image of two men having sex makes them feel very horny. So far, the male homosexual porn industry has been the only access for us to see really good-looking guys

Many women as well as gay men like to watch boy/boy scenes.

acting very masculine and magnificent. I have many gay fans who tell me they like my work because I only film good-looking men and because I encourage them to show off their personality.

There is a very distinct difference between how the male body is perceived in heterosexual and gay pornography. In heterosexual films, any focus on the man is almost by-passed in favour of the woman, and the male counterpart is often treated as little more than a mobile erection. You may get a fleeting glimpse of his backside as the camera pans by.

In gay films, the emphasis is either more on the erection and anus – which if they are the continual focus can be offputting for women – or on the man's looks. So decide what you like in gay films; consider the things you like about your man; and accentuate them. Think about how he makes you feel, whether you want him on top or underneath, and whether you want him to dress up.

In gay films, the look of an actor often defines the type of sex that he enacts. You can almost tell what type of sex an actor is going to have simply by his hairstyle. For example, in a scene with a blue-collar beefcake and a doe-eyed boy new to town, the doe-eyed boy is always the one that gets shafted, and the beefcake is the one that shafts. It would be good to see it the other way around, with the beefcake instructing the boy on how to do it to him. You don't have to look like the porn stereotype, and you can play with the stereotypes in more original ways too, such as reversing their roles.

Some gay films have almost no lead-up to the sex – like a lot of heterosexual adult movies. When you are

filming think about slowly removing your clothes for each other and the camera. Take the time to look at your man's body and admire it. Don't rush it, because these lingering shots show the body worship, which will be sustained throughout the whole film. Without it you have to imagine their body in a fully worshipped glory.

The all-over treatment

Think about how you take your clothes off, slowing it down and teasing. Even if you don't normally do this in your sex life, on film it will make you look much more impressive if you take them off in a confident manner. Men also look good with their T-shirts pinning their arms up and behind their heads.

When you are filming each other, it is important to remember to film faces as well as bodies. A pan down from the face to the body will remind you whose body is whose. This is especially important if you and your man both have similar body types. It can get very confusing and a bit disorienting if you film two bodies without having a head in the frame.

You know what type of pornography you usually buy, whether it is story-led or wall-to-wall anal sex. So it's important to think what type of feel you want to give your film. Is it in the style of 'Bel Ami' or trashy S & M? Are you in awe of the beauty of your partner or the hardness of the action? It is difficult to film both successfully at the same time. You can incorporate all the ideas discussed in earlier chapters in your film: food, props, clothes, locations and so on. Try incorporating vacuum pumps, cock rings and dildos too. Glass tabletops also give you interesting shots from underneath.

Some positions which look good in gay films are:
- 69
- Male daisy chain – several men performing oral sex on each other.
- Missionary – with legs over the shoulders.
- Rimming – with legs over the shoulders.
- Anal – both standing straight up against a wall or lying flat on the floor, legs slightly spread.
- Masturbation – by another man while you are in a rolled-up ball.

Don't forget all the erogenous zones. If you like total all-over body stimulation, then go ahead and film it. Just because the average gay erotic movie doesn't include it, this doesn't mean you shouldn't – it's all about what turns you on, after all. If that's what you want, this is your chance to make your own specialized film, incorporating all the elements that you enjoy.

Safe sex

When I ask people what they would like to see on film, I am often told that there is not enough erotic safe sex available. We all still have safe sex etched in our minds as being responsible and therefore not fun. You can use a condom without showing it, however, or you can incorporate it into your scene as a prop. Whatever you decide, there is no excuse for letting it get in the way of your fun. I have always shot a large proportion of my films using condoms and I really don't see a problem. It is true that condom sex lacks some of the sensitivity of condom-free sex, but I feel you should be able to by-pass that fact mentally when you are getting off together on a video. Some gay directors cut off the rim of the condom so that it is less visible, but obviously this has safety implications. Generally, I think you should simply not focus on the condom. Just use it and don't let it get in the way of your fun. If I can make it work professionally, then you can make it work at home.

Foreplay, props and mutual masturbation comes into play when shooting girl/girl scenes.

Equipment

So, you are feeling confident that you really want to be porn stars. Unfortunately, while the sex is free, the equipment you need in order to film it is not. However, as long as you have a modern camera, you don't necessarily have to spend very much on optional accessories.

Why not treat your camera as a new sex toy?

Equipment

Many people these days have access to some sort of video camera, whether it is VHS, SVHS, Video 8, Hi8, digital 8 or Mini DV. Most models on the market are pretty foolproof, allowing you to simply point and shoot without really needing to understand how the camera works. You can also get by without buying any accessories like a tripod, specialist lens, additional microphone or editing equipment.

In this section, I offer information on how to get started with the basic equipment, as well as advice to help you decide whether you want to invest in a range of technical accessories or whether you want to make do with items around the home.

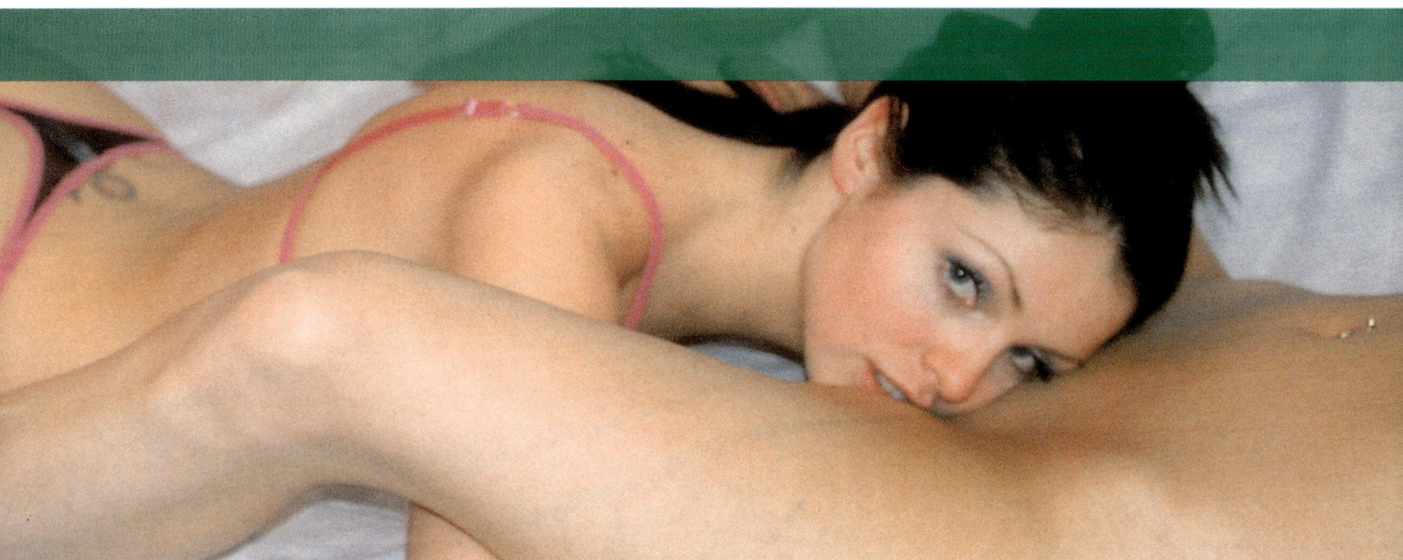

I will also explain the basic workings of each piece of equipment works so that you have the choice, either now or at some future date, to put the camera into manual mode, as opposed to automatic, and start making your films look that extra bit more impressive. There are many adjustable functions that will give your movie completely different characteristics and give you much greater control of how your final film looks. Even though you may well decide not to go and show the finished movie to everyone you know, it's always nice to think that they would be impressed if they ever did see your masterpiece.

Alongside each section of explanations, you will find a quick-start box containing all the necessary information if you do feel the need to jump straight in.

CAMERA

When you pick up a video camcorder, you will find under the menu settings or in the instruction manual that there are many options for changing the appearance of the image you shoot. Some of these involve adjusting the manual setting – focus, zoom, F-stop, gain, sound levels and aperture – and some deal with picture effects or filters that you can apply to the image.

Basic camera technique

The home-video camera is made to be as easy as possible to use in its basic functions. You can literally turn it on and point it at your partner and 99 percent of the time the

Most cameras enable you to start filming straight away.

result will be fine. If you are eager to get started with your erotic masterpiece, this may well be all you wish to do. You can make perfectly good movies this way – I shot in automatic mode for the first 30 or so programmes I made professionally, and there were no complaints. It does have to be said, however, that not many porn fans phone in about the merits of using manual focus! I found that there were advantages to being spontaneous, which helped me to learn about the genre and how to film a good performance. So go and do it. But before you do, let me point out a few basics to help you maintain a good image.

Quick-start camera hints for automatic cameras

- If you want to move the camera around, in order to do a pan up your partner's body, for example, do it slowly; this will give the autofocus time to adjust and prevents the camera being 'thrown' out of focus at any time. You don't have to be too slow – a quick practice will give you some idea.
- If your partner is silhouetted against a light background – standing in front of a day-lit window, for instance – either move your position so that the light source is no longer behind them, or zoom into your partner's body so the window no longer dominates the frame.
- Try to avoid shooting in situations where daylight and artificial light are both present in the same shot, for example, looking down a hallway towards the open front door. (Although, you might not want to know all about how light works and how it can make you look less attractive, I do advise you to have a look at the quick-start box in the lighting section.)
- Always zoom in and out slowly, otherwise the autofocus will not be able to keep up.
- When moving in very close to your partner, zoom the lens out to its widest point (W) and then physically move in. The camera will be able to maintain focus much nearer to your subject.

Advanced camera technique

You may find using the manual settings on your camera a bit difficult at first, especially if you have no previous experience of photography. But I am confident that, with a bit of practice and a lot of mistakes, you will soon get the hang of it. There are six main functions that will help you to achieve a better picture.

1. Focus

As I've said previously, I shoot porn in autofocus most of the time. Generally, if a scene is lit adequately, the camera will maintain its focus accurately enough. Bear in mind that the alternative is to have one hand working continually on the focus, thus having no hands free to zoom or push someone's knees out the way. (Many porn directors like to keep their right hand free for other uses!)

The only times that I might use manual focus are either when I'm shooting in a dark situation where the camera can't see what to focus on, or when I need to film a scene in which the action moves from the background into the foreground and needs to be immediately in focus. An example of this would be an empty doorway in which someone suddenly appears. In this instance, autofocus would initially focus beyond the doorway, possibly on a far wall, and then visibly and relatively slowly adjust itself, far to near, when a person comes through the door and into the foreground, and this would spoil your artistic shot.

2. Exposure

You can adjust the exposure to compensate for low and high light levels (under-exposure and over-exposure); for example, an external shot at night, or where the image is bleached out. Sometimes a shot will have both very dark and very light areas – in the case of a person standing in front of a sunlit window. If you do not increase exposure on the person you will not be able to see their features. However, increasing the amount of exposure in order to see the face will ultimately mean that a really bright window will become over-exposed. But this is still the preferred option.

Some cameras feature a 'zebra pattern', which activates when an area of a shot is over-exposed, and registers that area in your viewfinder as a striped 'blob'. You can then lower the exposure until the 'zebra' area disappears. It is worth remembering that, in doing so, you may make other areas of the shot too dark, so it is a matter of balancing the two options.

Autofocus lets you have one hand free so that you can be involved in the action.

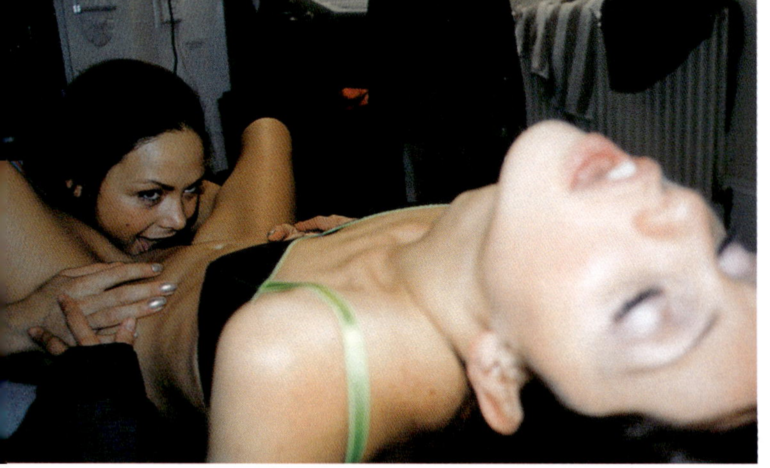

3. F-stop

Changing the F-stop means changing the 'depth of field', which the camera does by opening or closing its iris. Depth of field refers to how much of your shot is in complete focus – in other words, to what degree the objects in front of and behind your subject are in focus to the same extent as that subject. A low 'F-number' (large iris) will create a short focal range with little more than the subject in focus, while a high 'F-number' will result in a long focal range so the majority of the shot will be in focus as well as your subject. Need an example? Thought you might.

You have two women at each end of the bed and in between them you have a dildo. If we take the dildo as the subject – the point on which we focus our camera – and chose a low F-stop, only the dildo will be in focus. Conversely, a high F-stop would mean all three subjects would be in focus.

You can play with depth of field to tell a story and to imply relationships between elements in your image. For example, if you set the point of focus between the dildo and one of the models, bringing the dildo and only one of the models into focus, that model will look as if she owns, or is after the dildo, because the illusion of space created implies that she has an association with the dildo.

Is there an advantage to having some things out of focus? Isn't it better that everything is sharp? The answer is 'No', for one very good reason. The retina in the human eye is made of thousands of focal sensors, which tell us how far away objects are from us. Among these sensors there is only one sharp focus sensor based right in the middle, while the rest are all soft focus, located all around the back of the eye. This is so that we can be selective about what we focus on.

Look straight ahead and focus on one object and, without moving your eyes, think about how the objects all around it are at varying degrees of soft focus, radiating out from the centre, and getting progressively more out of focus the further they are from the focused object. So, if you shoot with a fairly low F-number like F5.6, the resulting image will have a more 'realistic feel' because it looks more the way we are used to seeing.

Be careful not to go below F5.6 as the quality of the colours can suffer. The next time you watch a film, see how much of the image is in soft focus.

4. White balance

This adjustment makes white objects look white. I'll explain. Different types of light cast different colours onto white objects (and everything else too) and while we don't notice it, the camera does. Artificial indoor lighting casts an orange colour and daylight casts a blue colour. Most domestic cameras give you a choice of setting that allows you to move between 'indoor' and 'outdoor' manually. So you would change the white balance when you move from inside a house to outdoors. The automatic white-balance option is usually very reliable, however, and I would settle with what it suggests unless your image looks peculiar.

5. Shutter speed

Your camera may have a function which allows you to change the speed at which the shutter opens and shuts – it will probably range from 1/4 to 1/10,000. 'Normal' shutter speed is around 1/50. Adjusting the speed to a much slower rate will create a strobe effect, whereby you will slowly change frames, rather like individual photos or CCTV footage. Unless you want to use it as a special effect, you don't really need to adjust the shutter speed for your purposes.

You should be able to 'lock' all these manual functions so that you can handle the camera without fear of knocking the settings off by accident. A good camera will enable you to view the settings in your viewfinder, so that you know what you are using at all times.

6. Picture effects

Cameras that have been developed for the home user come with quite a selection of effects that you can activate simply by pressing a button, and the image changes to your chosen effect without affecting the sound. Examples include 'old movie', 'trail', 'negative', 'black and white', 'stretch' and 'slim'. Many of these effects can also be added at the editing stage using specialist software (see Chapter 8, 'Editing').

It is worth remembering that these effects allow you to add a comic effect (stretch/slim), for example, or suggest a past time (old movie, sepia) as part of your movie. However, such effects, if used in the wrong place, tend to distract the viewer's attention – from the romping action and onto the effect. Try not to include them in the actual sex scenes as they rarely enhance the sex. Also, avoid using the 'stretch' function on your lover's backside unless they have a very good sense of humour!

CAMERA CARE

If you are generally careful when using and storing your camera, you will avoid any major problems with it and probably only have to replace it when it's superseded by a better model. However, there are a few precautions you can take to help prevent any damage to your machine.

General camera maintenance

Keep your lens clean using a hand-operated air syringe or air can held 30cm away from the lens. Greasy fingermarks can be removed using lens fluid on a lens tissue. Use a head cleaning cassette every ten times you film for ten seconds only at a time – don't use more often or for longer as they work by removing a thin layer of the camera head.

Special conditions

- Cold – extreme cold can damage your camera but all cold will reduce the power of your batteries. Use either a specialist insulating cover or a carefully placed coat!
- Heat – avoid leaving your camera for any length of time near a radiator, in direct or indirect sunlight, in the boot of a car on a hot day, or too near the lights. Sunlight can be reflected by specialist silver sun/dust covers or a clean white T-shirt.
- Wet – rain, steam, bathwater and water spray from a hose are all to be avoided. Protect your camera by using professional rain covers, a thick rubbish bag (preferably see-through) with holes cut for the eyepiece and lens, or just an umbrella. Don't attempt to submerge your camera in water unless you use a specialist housing.
- Air – moist, salty, dusty or sandy air can all cause havoc. Avoid these situations or use a specialist cover.

All covers are available from professional hire shops – or check the Internet and the back pages of photography magazines. Covers may create unwanted sound, especially while hand-operating, so in these cases use your camera remote control if there is one.

Skin tone looks different under daylight (left above) as opposed to artificial light (left below).

TRIPODS

A tripod is used to steady the camera. A decent tripod gives a firm and secure base on which to fix your camera, enabling you to leave it attached and running, freeing up your hands for other things. You can be sure that the camera will be safe from damage unless it is interfered with; for example, if you get carried away and accidentally kick it over. Tripods also help to steady camera movements, such as:

- Pan – a movement generally from left to right or vice versa, although you can pan up and down. It is used to link two elements. For example, a man enters a room and the camera follows him to the telephone on the far side of the set, which was originally out of shot.

- Tracking shot – you can buy equipment such as a dolly, a skid or skate from more specialist video/photographic shops for this, which you use with a tripod. This is a piece of equipment with wheels which keeps the legs of a tripod at a fixed position but allows you to move the camera around the set. It is ideal for following a person from one room to another with the viewpoint over their shoulder. The floor has to be very smooth for this shot to work well as any small bump on the floor will be magnified considerably.
- Zoom – a tripod keeps a camera completely still, so you will be able to zoom in far more smoothly, moving right up close to your subject without the shot suffering from the inevitable camera shake when it is hand-held. Zoom is especially effective if your camera comes with a remote control.

Do I really need to buy a tripod?

The short answer is 'No', if you don't want to. There is no need to invest in a tripod if you are not really concerned about whether a shot is at exactly the right height, position or angle. There are always alternative ways to mount a camera, but I would say that a tripod does give you one less thing to think about while you get on with the sex – and for a relatively small cost. Here are some alternatives to use instead of a tripod:

- Chair – it must be level to the scene, though – i.e. at the same height from the ground as your bed.
- Pile of books – these are handy because you can build them to any height, but they can be kicked over easily.
- Shelf – these are useful because they come at different heights. However, it's not often that the shelf's position is just in line with the bed/sex area with a view to shooting a sex scene, but you might strike lucky.
- Wardrobe – good for that 'security CCTV' look, but securing it in a downward position can be a problem and you would have to put the camera on the nearest corner pointing downwards at an acute angle unless you are shooting in a very large room and your subject is a reasonable distance away.
- Drinks trolley, barbecue stand or shopping cart – you can use any number of moving objects to create amusing tracking shots.

Whichever support you choose, you need to find a way to fix your camera to it. This can be done with mouldable mounting adhesive or a with adhesive tapes. Be sure that the camera is secured in all directions and that you are not damaging the camera itself or the support.

Which tripod should I buy?

As with most things, you get what you pay for. Tripods and camera bases can cost as much as, if not more than, the camera itself, and the shots they help you create can be amazing. They use several different methods, such as pneumatic pressure and counter weights, to achieve controllable shots. But to start you off, there are four features you should look for when you're purchasing a tripod: weight and sturdiness (generally the heavier the better, although very heavy tripods can be cumbersome); locking parts (all moving parts should fully 'lock off' so you can secure it firmly in position); smooth pan and tilt (a 'liquid head' compensates for your jerky movements); and a good spirit level.

A few hints on using a tripod

- When attaching the camera, first fix the plate to the camera with the arrow pointing in the direction of the lens and then attach both to the tripod. If at any time you can't find the plate, in my experience the first place to look is on the bottom of the camera.
- When you initially attach your camera to the tripod, *hold onto only the camera*, and give it a gentle shake, to make sure it is secure.
- ALWAYS support your camera with your hand underneath the lens when fixing it to, or releasing it from, the tripod. It can spin off the panhead (the part to which your camera is fixed to the tripod) extremely quickly when you release the plate lock.
- When changing the tilt knob (the knob that allows the camera to go up and down) make sure that you support the camera with one hand because the weight of the lens will always cause it to swing downwards.

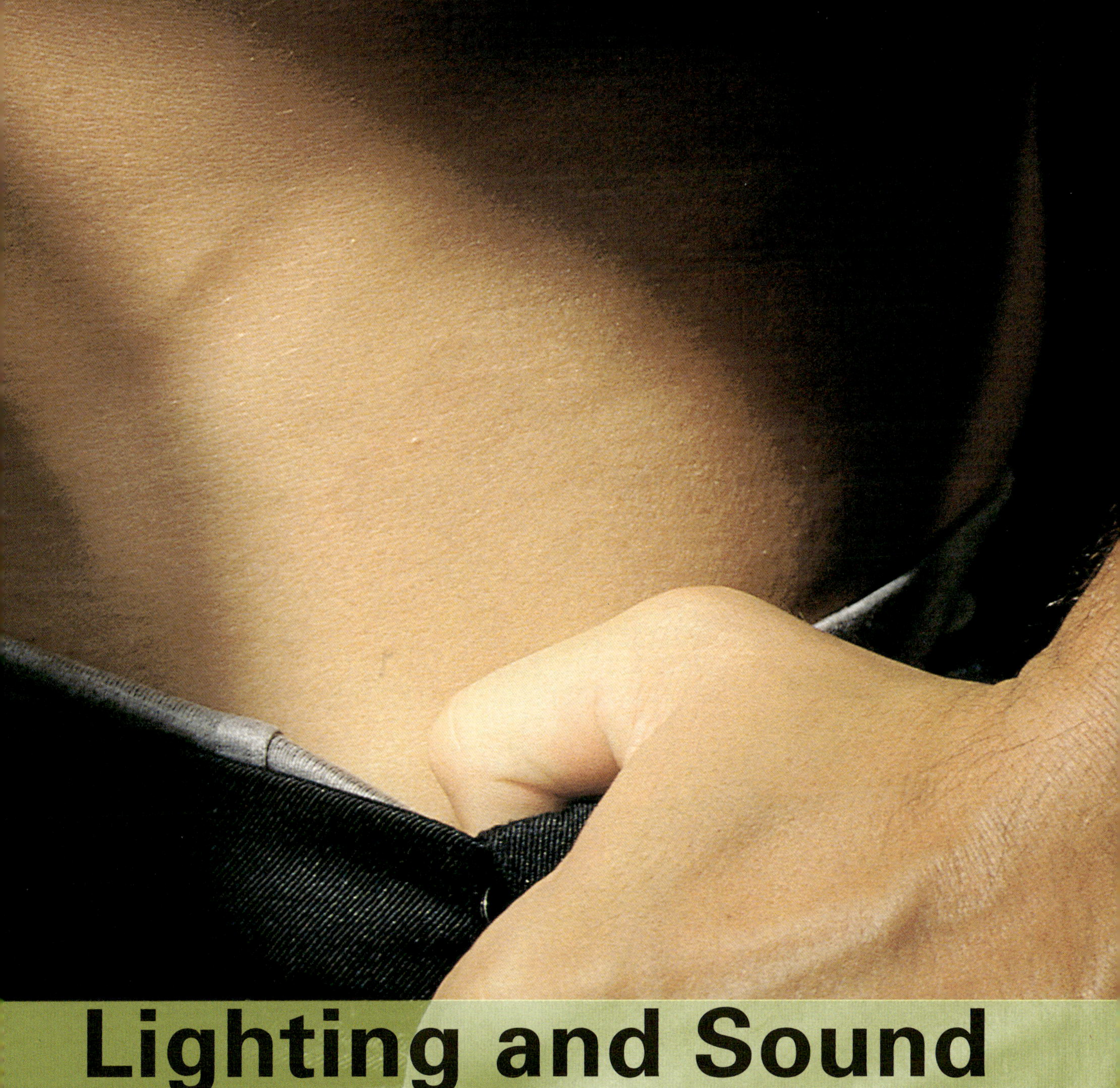

Lighting and Sound

Using the correct lighting for your erotic movie not only enables you to see all the sexy details when you play it back, but it will help to make you look your porn-star best. Along with music and sound, lighting also enhances the mood of the film.

Light and sound are as vital as the actors. Without them you see and hear nothing.

Lighting and Sound

Good lighting makes a huge influence on the visual content and atmosphere of your film. If you prefer not to buy lights, you can always hire them from professional specialist companies who stock everything you will need for a photo shoot. You can find the details of your nearest hire shop on the web or in the back of most video or photographic magazines. Among the other lights you can use are your normal household lights, bedside or portable lamps, external/camping lamps and torches (flashlights). Even ordinary lights can be used to create special effects.

To make as good a start as possible, I suggest using two 300-watt lights and one 500-watt light, so that you can set up basic three-way lighting (see pages 101–4), one of the simplest but most effective methods. The higher the wattage, the more expensive the lights become, but this is probably a strong enough set-up for an average-sized room. Another type of light available is the Photoflood. It is a bulb that fits directly into a normal household bulb fitting, but is much stronger than your average 60-watt bulb. They are easy to use and can be bought in most photographic shops, but beware. Because of the strength of the light, Photofloods generate a lot more heat, so never use one in a lamp with a plastic socket and make sure that any shade on the lamp is a safe distance from the bulb.

BASIC LIGHTING

The poor lighting of commercial adult movies is a common cause for complaint. A badly lit film makes everyone look terrible. Even the most beautiful performers can look unattractive if the lighting technician job hasn't been done properly. The most common mistakes include using the wrong colour light, ignoring shadows and putting the light much too close to a model, or in the wrong place completely.

Basically, the more light you put into the room, the more you will be able to see in the final film. Digital cameras have the ability to see in some very dark situations (more so than Hi8 and VHS), but the darker the room, the more 'grainy' and lacking in clarity the image will

Lighting can have a significant effect on the mood and atmosphere of your final film.

The first is what I call the 'glossy look', which originated in the United States in the early 1980s. It looks very bright (technically over-lit), but soft (diffused), with no obvious shadows. The light is often warm in colour, giving skin tones a peach/honey glow. The effect of this light is to hide skin blemishes and cellulite. Shiny make-up and body glitter can also make the most of the light. Perfect hair and make-up are used to give the illusion that the models have 'super-real', perfect bodies. But it has an artificial quality that makes the narrative difficult to believe, as it is immediately obvious that this is a studio set-up. Nevertheless, it can be quite enough if there is a pretty model with shiny lip gloss and diamondy nails with a super stud getting down to it.

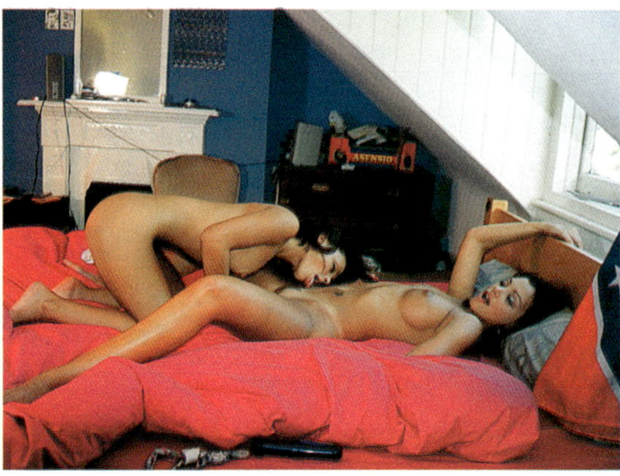

be. The same is true with all film and video. Low light also adversely affects the speed of the autofocus function. If you can see a grainy effect in your viewfinder, then the effect will feature in your final film too. So light it well.

Lighting in commercial adult movies

You wouldn't know it to look at the majority of porn, but film lighting is all about placing shadows to create the illusion of reality. A good lighting director (LD) looks at a script and thinks of ways to create the correct lighting set-up to suit the specific scenario. If the scene looks real, the viewer momentarily forgets that they are watching a fictional story. Whether or not a viewer empathizes with the character is as much to do with the lighting as with the actor's ability or director's vision. It is difficult to get immersed in a plot if, subconsciously, you are aware that the story is taking place in a studio. An LD must imitate reality so that we do not notice any lighting at all, whether it is an external daylight situation, an underground nightclub with no natural light, or a room in a house with both natural and artificial household light. (Special effects and fantasy situations have slightly different criteria.)

In today's adult entertainment industry, there are two basic types of lighting. Both have their own appeal.

The second type of lighting (and film) is the naturalistic amateur style of the 'girl next-door', often referred to as the 'Gonzo' style (see box opposite, and page 118). This style first became fashionable in the early to mid-1990s and emerged while the camcorder was being developed in response to the over-stylized, glossy, unreal porn genre. It now accounts for around 50 percent of all films and programmes sold. A common storyline involves a camera-man picking up a girl on the street and persuading her to have sex in front of the camera in her house. The emphasis is on realism, so natural and existing ambient light, i.e. domestic lights, are often all that are used. The result is a set-up that is, performance willing, more believable. However, it is also often unflattering, as this lighting does not necessarily exaggerate the model's beauty; it has been utilized for ease and for the sense of reality.

I asked my friend Steve Perry, also known as Ben Dover, Britain's most successful adult movie exporter, where the term Gonzo had come from. Apparently, it was coined by *Leaving Las Vegas* author, Hunter S Thompson. While he was working as a sports reporter for a US newspaper, he was watching a dull baseball match and realized that he could liven things up and create a story if he caused a commotion by tripping up the popcorn seller. He termed this style 'Gonzo', and porn took on the idea wholeheartedly. Gonzo became the term to describe a camera-man who intervenes from behind the camera to change the events in front of it.

I have always maintained in my films that believability is very important but, commercially speaking, attractive models are, too. So I opt for a style that is halfway between the two types of lighting, so that it is both realistic and has a hint of glamour. In order to achieve this it is important to understand the basics of lighting from positioning the lamps; the difference between hard and soft light and how to use them; and what is meant by 'colour temperature'.

POSITIONING

Naturalistic lighting is based on the idea that our primary source of light is the sun. Although there may be many other light sources, such as electric lamps or sunlight reflected from a car door, these sources of illumination are secondary.

Basic three-way lighting

This is a simple arrangement of three lamps. The 'key light' imitates the sun, so it should be the highest wattage (500 watt) of the three, and also the light that determines the position of any other lights used. If you use more than one main key light, you will automatically create a more unrealistic scene, because it will look unnatural.

Where do you put the key light? That depends on what you are filming. For example, the best place to put the light in a sit-down interview is in almost the same position as the camera. You would want to illuminate the 'smaller' side of the interviewee's face (we are nearly all lopsided, I'm afraid) because the reflected light would make it seem larger (light is more fattening than dark, as all 'little black dress' owners know). We are trying to light an adult movie set, however, where the whole point is movement, so you have to light your 'set' with that in mind. Ideally, you need to create a lighting situation that will look good in most shots and that will enable you to forget the lighting once it is set up in order to get on with the important things, like sex.

As an example, let's take a domestic house interior with a large window on one wall and a bed in the centre, where the action will take place. This room had better be upstairs if you are shooting in daylight (or you are going to attract some attention from passers-by). Your key light is the sun coming through the window. If the sunlight is changeable, you should position your key light directly in front of the window to support the daylight and thereby keep it constant. Position the light as high up as possible to replicate the angle of the sun.

Now when you turn on your key light, it will create strong shadows. This is the reason for your second light, your 'fill light' (300 watt). The point of the fill light is, literally, to fill in the shadows caused by the key light. You should position your fill light directly opposite the key. Because it is not as strong as the key, it will not cause problem shadows.

The third light is called the 'back light' (300 watt). This is used to counteract the way the key light removes depth from a scene. If you don't add a back light your figures may look flat against the background, with no shadows to differentiate them from it. The back light should be high, and should point down to light the back of the subject.

Exactly the same arrangement can be employed in a situation with no natural daylight. Just keep the camera's white-balance set to 'indoor', and don't use any daylight gels on the lights.

If you find this too complicated, try angling all three lamps upwards so that light bounces off the ceiling (but only if your ceiling is white). This will diffuse the light, making it spread over a much wider area, and giving you an even overall light, rather like the glossy type of

If you are working on a budget, three-way lighting gives the most professional-looking results.

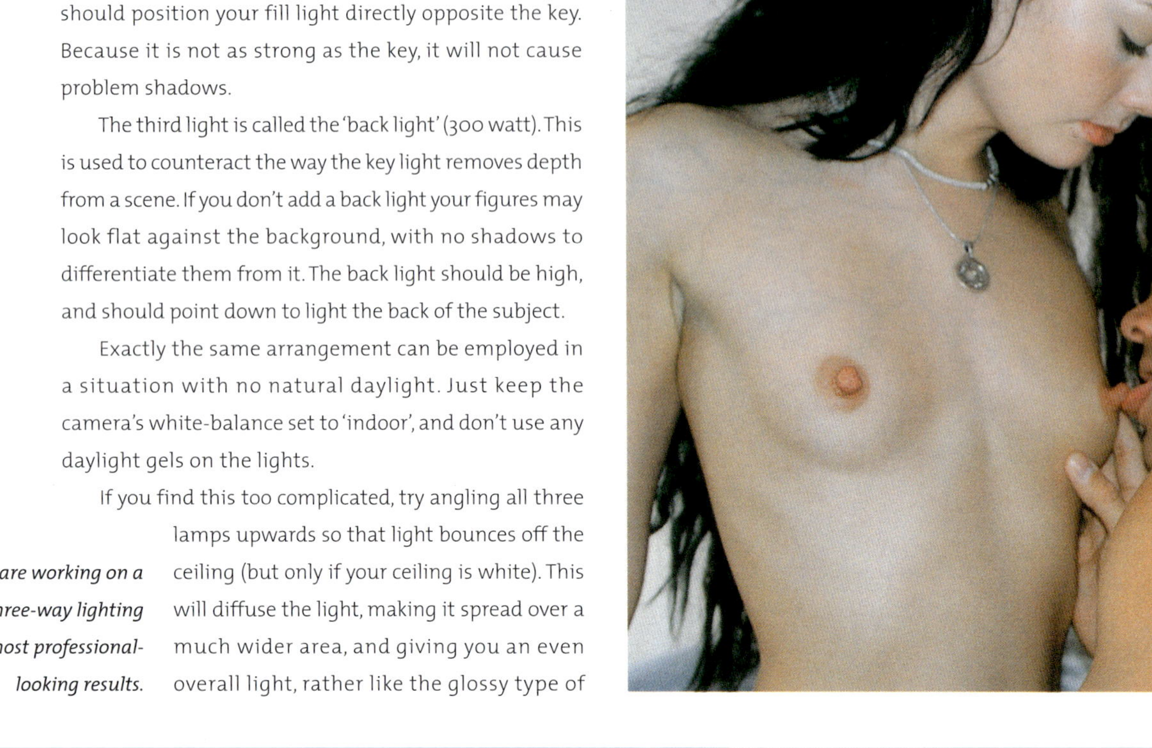

adult movie. Because it reduces the three-dimensional effect created by the three-way lighting system, it looks less realistic, but the bonus is that it will get rid of your cellulite (not in real life, you understand).

One definite 'no-no' of shooting flesh is to light from the floor upwards. When I was a tender, physically unconfident teenager, I remember once having the shock of my life. I was in my bedroom, with everything strewn across the floor. I had a large mirror leaning against the wall opposite my TV, which was also on the floor, pointing towards the ceiling. There was a 1940s black-and-white horror movie on and, as I stepped out of bed, I caught sight of the reflection of my bare legs in the mirror. Now my legs don't have much cellulite, but what a sight! The flickering light made the back of my legs look like they were covered in bumps. As I looked down at the TV there was a woman staring up, gripping her face, screaming. I felt like joining in. The moral is: don't light directly from above or below.

Hard and soft lighting

Basically, a hard light is a direct light that uses no diffusing tool. The sun is the most natural hard and directional source of light, and it can cast strong shadows, but when there are clouds in front of the sun they act as diffusers, softening the shadows by dispersing the light throughout the sky.

You can buy diffusers from most photographic shops. It is possible to use greaseproof paper, but do remember to keep it way away from the light because it may catch fire. You could also attach a white bed sheet to a frame and place it in front of the light on a stand, but again be aware of the potential fire hazard.

Style your lighting to suit the mood of your film, whether it be a fun movie, or set in a seedy dungeon.

Use colour temperature gels to complement the existing light conditions.

effect, but in film and video you can't. Combining types of light will make the image look messy and unreal. And your actors won't look at all alluring.

So what do you do if you are shooting inside with the lights on and there is sunlight coming through the window? You cheat. You make the two light sources the same type of colour by altering one of them to suit the other. The easiest way to do this is to buy Colour Temperature Blue (CTB) gels and clip them loosely to the light with metal clips (allowing room for heat to escape the light) this changes the orange light to blue. (The alternative is to buy a bigger piece of Colour Temperature Orange (CTO) gel in order to cover all the window surfaces, so that it changes the blue daylight to an orange colour to match the domestic/ artificial lights. This comes with problems: keeping the gel out of shot and the cost of the gel.)

Set your camera's white balance to the right setting to match the lighting conditions. In the viewfinder menu, under white balance, there will be a little logo, usually a light bulb, for indoor artificial light, and usually the sun, for daylight. Either select the right one yourself, or set it to auto, and let the camera figure it out.

Points to remember when using lights

- If you are using any sort of light stand, you have to keep in mind where they are when you are filming so as not to include them inadvertently in shot and also so as not to walk into them, either backwards or sideways. It's very easy to do, especially if you are turned on, and it can be dangerous, especially if you are naked.

- For safety, always keep an electrical household fire extinguisher near you in the room in case of fire. Also, if making this film takes a long time, turn the lights off to allow them to cool down when you take a break.

- If you are resting the lights on anything, make sure it is fireproof.

- Don't position the lights too closely to yourselves. It is very easy to kick a light over in the heat of the moment and lights get extremely hot.

- Professional gels and diffusers are made to withstand intense heat, and even they regularly melt. Keep any substitutes away from the bulbs, and avoid angling

If you use a professional diffuser, don't use plastic clothespegs to attach it to your lamp, because they melt.

It is also possible to soften hard light by reflecting it off a surface, and thereby dispersing the resulting light. You can bounce light at an angle off a white wall, a large piece of polystyrene, a white sheet or a ceiling. Or you can buy special reflecting equipment quite cheaply from photographic shops.

Colour temperature

Without getting too technical, all light that is not deliberately coloured – with a red gel, say – is part of a scale that ranges from orange (low-colour temperature) to blue (high-colour temperature). Domestic light tends more to the orange end of the scale and natural daylight is bluer. In photography you can use both artificial and natural light in the same shot to create any desired gels and diffusers above the lamp so as to prevent the heat escaping from the light, as this could cause them to catch fire.

- If your room has brightly coloured walls, light may bounce off them. Red walls would cast a red glow onto both of you, making you look like lobsters. Therefore, try to position the lights so that they don't face any walls. You may have to bounce the light off the ceiling, presuming it's white. If the ceiling is red as well I would suggest re-writing the script to incorporate the look – possibly to a devil and sinner scenario, or maybe a king lobster and naughty prawn (shrimp) tale.

Creative lighting

The three-point lighting set-up is supposed to recreate a natural look. However, you may want to create a

white light, angled directly onto your partner tied to a chair, to imply an interrogation situation (... ooh make him confess, the bad boy).

You can also use external garden lights – the string of bulbs type – or security lights, many of which can be set to stay on for ten minutes after sensing movement, so that they are effectively on all the time. But be extremely careful about the fire risks involved, especially inside the house. If you are using a wet set, by a swimming pool or in the bathroom, for example, external waterproof lights may also be preferable.

You might like to consider using a torch (flashlight) as the only source of light in a pitch-black room, or even the camera's own infra-red setting, if it has one. You could make quite an amazing scene involving a hunt for the other person who, if found, has to submit to whatever

more dynamic or stylized look. You can create a lot of atmosphere using coloured gels. For example, a red gel can imply a red-light district for a prostitute fantasy. A green gel could be an alien space rape scenario, if that is your thing. Or you may want to use a single bright-

you desire. It could have quite a build-up, especially if you have to hunt all around the house first and genuinely don't know where your partner is or what they might be doing – a kind of adult hide and seek.

Be aware of where your lights are because wayward limbs can easily knock them over.

With this type of lighting it is inevitable that the image will suffer some graininess because the scene is so dark. You can either accept it as part of the 'feel' of the scene – the *Blair Witch* of adult movies – or you can increase the exposure to improve the situation. Autofocus will also work less effectively in the dark, but it is all part of the look, so don't worry about it.

> I once shot a film about a friend of mine being seduced by a strange lady, who simply appeared out of nowhere at a New Year's Eve firework display on a crowded London heath. As I approached the heath to shoot the scene, I noticed that a mysterious fog had suddenly arrived, and I realized it would just as quickly disappear. So I stuck my camera onto 'auto everything' and filmed this haunting woman standing completely still, staring straight at my friend, from inside the fog. It would have looked like a classic 1940s *Film Noir* – a glamourous lady in the Chicago mist – had it not been for the combination of the autofocus struggling to keep up and the hand-held camera movement. But the point is that the shot was still worth using and still appears in the final film – *Anna's Xmas*.

SOUND

After the visual stimulation that we get from erotic movies, sound is the next most important element, and can be the factor which decides whether we believe and involve ourselves in the action, or not.

All films are half-sound and half-vision, but the cinema-going population often overlook the importance of sound in a film. Sound can decide whether we believe the narrative. For example, imagine there are two people walking swiftly through an office and talking very fast to each other. The camera is focused on them, possibly only framing their head and shoulders. You don't see much of the background, but the feeling is of a very busy work environment. Why? Because the director has supported the shot with ambient office noise and recordings of people on telephones, opening and closing doors, rustling paper, computers and so on, making the overall effect much more believable.

I'm not suggesting that you go out with a microphone and recording machine to collect ambient road noise to back up your traffic warden – cheeky driver scenario, but if you give some consideration to sound at this point, it might throw up some ideas that will enhance your fantasy portrayals.

It is also worth taking into account the fact that sound can sometimes detract from your enjoyment when you are watching a film. For example, if you film a chat-up situation on the side of a busy road and you have to strain your ears to hear anything, your attention will be concentrated away from your groin and in your head, which is not the desired effect at all. Similarly, if you are getting down to some sizzling sex and all you can hear is children playing in the background through an open window, this may affect your mood as well.

When I shoot I use a professional external camera-mounted microphone because it gives good sound quality in a small and easy-to-handle unit. You can achieve better sound quality using a boom and rifle microphone, or a clip-on tie microphone, but these are more cumbersome when you want to get really close to the action. It can also be a problem trying to find a place to clip a tie microphone on a naked person!

Camera sound quality

The microphone on your camera will be good enough to pick up the sound for your film, but if you want to invest a little bit more, you can buy a camera-mounted microphone from most photographic shops. However, occasionally when you widen the shot, you may see the end of the microphone in the frame. You can buy a cheap accessory called a PC adaptor to help get around this minor problem: it attaches to the camera to add height to your microphone.

You really don't need to worry too much about the sound in your film from a technical point of view. Most models of camera allow you to monitor and change your

sound levels in the menu if you feel that the sound is too low, or distorted because it is too high. Auto levels, especially on digital cameras, are usually very good.

Moreover, there are a lot of aspects of sound that you can think about and play with that will increase your creative flexibility and improve your film immensely.

Dialogue

This is one aspect of adult film-making that I love and think is often overlooked. The use of speech in a sexual environment can be electrifying. A performer who can not only give a great physical performance but who also has the confidence and skill to talk though a sex scene is the best type of performer. Some people are better at it than others, but I believe that it is a lot to do with practice and having the guts to give it a go. There's no doubt that the idea of talking during sex can seem very daunting, but like most things, you can start off small and extend yourself, taking risks as your confidence grows.

Before your actual sex scene starts you can use dialogue to establish your characters. Spend three or four minutes in character – as a plumber and a housewife talking through the problems with the washing machine, even making him a cup of tea while you chat. Getting into the character paves the way for a really good sex scene, allowing you to build tension, to play with *double entendres* or to tease each other. Compare this to the normal porn movie in which the introduction often only lasts one minute, if you're lucky, before the funky music starts and the sex begins.

Why make noise?

Once again, this is to do with the five senses to two rule (see page 61). When you watch an erotic movie you can't experience the smells, tastes or feel of the scene, so in order to give yourselves as much information as possible to fill in the picture when it comes to watching the movie you need to over-compensate with the other two senses – sight and sound. Just as you exaggerate your movements physically, so you must increase your vocal levels to express, either in words or sounds, how you are feeling.

Being in character can make you more confident about talking or making noises in your sex scenes.

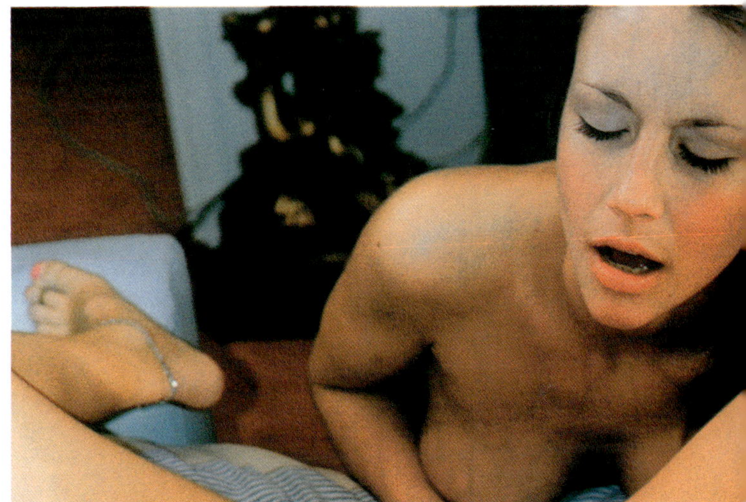

If you simply film yourself having sex as normal, without thinking about the sound and the positions, you will most likely get two people slumped over each other with very little discernible sound, even if the sex itself was an amazing experience. The physical feeling of penetration, oral stimulation, licking, kissing and so on, as well as the smells and tastes, just cannot be captured on video.

Porn performers are often mocked for their exaggerated noises and contorted positions. Sometimes it is true that they are unnecessarily over-emphasized, but the alternative – the depiction of sex without staging – is, quite simply, dull. You must be able to convey the physical feelings of sex, the taste and smell, through sound and vision alone, otherwise you are left with half a film.

If you don't feel very confident about talking on film, it is often much easier to be vocal if you are playing out your fantasy in character as this gives you the perfect excuse to talk dirty or make sexual noises you wouldn't normally feel comfortable about making.

Starting to make a noise

Don't think of making extra sexual noises as 'faking it'; think of it instead as 'outwardly expressing how you are feeling or what you are thinking' – letting your partner and the camera 'see' what is going on inside your head. Start by telling your partner what you like about them and what turns you on as they undress, or as they move in a sexual way, or look at you in a sexual manner. Just start with short, simple sentences.

Try asking your partner to do things that you like to see: for example, ask him or her to turn around or bend over so you can get a better view. Take it slowly. If you are the person answering the request, reply to you partner with comments like 'You mean... like this?' or 'Do you like the way I do that' as you bend over.

A good way to use dialogue is to create a feeling of anticipation. If you are a woman talking to her man while he masturbates for you, say something like 'I can't wait to feel that inside me.' Before you actually begin penetration, talk about the way his erection feels when he rubs it up and down inside you; where you can

feel it; what positions you would like him to put you in; how fast you want the pace to be; and so on. You can add to the excitement, by talking in a 'matter-of-fact' way, as the flatness of the tone can exaggerate the wildness of the actions you are asking him to perform on you. Keep eye contact on his erection and his face, going back and forth between the two. And be blasé with it as well. This works particularly well when you are acting out fantasy scenarios which involve an imbalance of power, such as a female boss telling the guy to do some extra overtime – possibly licking your envelopes.

Introduce dialogue into your movie either by playing out a scene or just talking dirty to each other.

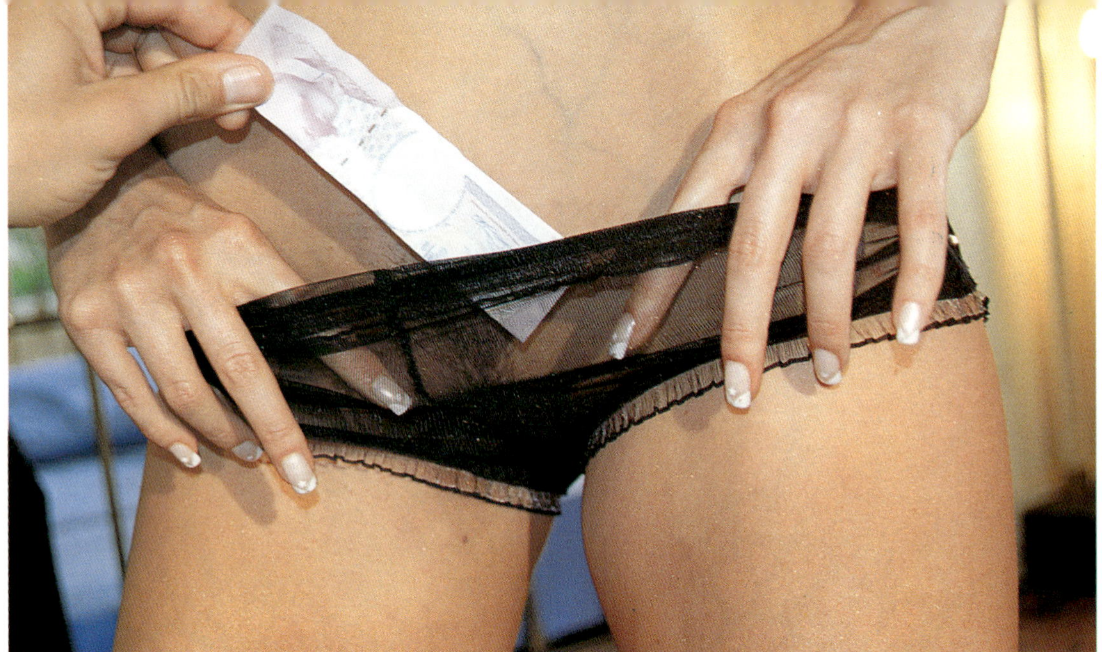

A similar example for a man taking the initiative would be to get a female partner to act as a paid prostitute over whom he has paid for control for the evening/hour. Don't underestimate the sensation of actually exchanging money during the scene – you can always give it back afterwards (although, if it were me, I probably wouldn't. You've got to have a sense of humour in a relationship).

The man has the right to ask for what he wants and the hooker must comply. In this situation, the man has a pre-planned secret scenario and can tell the hooker exactly how he wants her to make herself available for him – in which position, her facial expression, what she will say, right down to the angle of the hips and how wide she should spread her legs. The man should deliver this in a monologue, again in a matter-of-fact manner, perhaps in a lowered tone. He might leave the room to give her time to get ready, but will expect her to be in the required position when he comes back.

You can also use dialogue to express and heighten your pleasure while you are having sex. If you are caressing your partner's leg, for example, talk through the experience, telling them how their skin feels, and how they smell (this is not the time or the place for bad news). If you are enacting a fantasy involving specific characters, such as a schoolgirl and a teacher, then stay in character and use the appropriate language. The more 'realistic' the speech, the hotter the scene.

One way to start talking in bed if you are feeling self-conscious, is to mimic the 'bad porn' lines, such as 'Ooh boy, you are so...oo big' or 'Miss Stevens, can you come into my office, I've something I want you to take down.'

Exaggerating the 'ooohs', 'mmms' and 'aaahs' of sex can also add a great deal to a film. It is fashionable in porn to make the sort of noise you make when something looks painful – an intake of breath through almost closed teeth, with the air hitting the top of your mouth. It is supposed to imply that something is very sensitive in a nice way. Another fashion in adult movies is to exaggerate the slurping noises of a blow job,

literally making the mouth sound as though it is full of saliva, squelching and drooling. It roughly evokes the sounds of penetration.

But there is a thin line between sex noises sounding clear and sensuous, and the sex sounding farcical. If you feel like you are faking it, the chances are that the performance will look and sound rather false. But don't worry, you can learn to relax as you practise, until eventually you will feel more confident and able to express yourself naturally. If you are prepared to try, you can at least watch the films and have a good laugh at yourself. Keep on working at it until you find something that is sensual and evocative for both of you. There are worse things you could be doing with your spare time!

MUSIC

You can use any piece of music you like to accompany your erotic masterpiece because you are not releasing it for public consumption and therefore are not answerable to the record companies who release the tracks you use. (Sadly, I don't have that freedom. If I make money from using Michael Jackson's music in my film, some, or all of the money I make, should go to his record company.) But I should add that there could be legal complications if you release your film on the web. If this is your intention, I would suggest that you avoid having music in your movie.

So why use music?

A lot of music evokes primal urges, and so gives rhythm and has a sensual energy of its own. The rhythm of the music can hold a viewer's attention even when the sex lulls a bit. If the sex is not raunchy enough, then appropriate music will make it seem raunchier. If the sex is hot and pounding, then the repetition of a strong musical beat or rhythm will add to this energy.

Choosing your music

Basically, choose music you like, and music that reminds you of good times. It's a cliché, but some music has a totally sexy quality that other songs just don't have. A 'sassy' song can be the guide for your rhythm when

you strip. This is particularly true if you are feeling a bit nervous about stripping; let the music dictate your movements. The wrong choice of music can hinder your performance, making you feel awkward, even if your routine is well practised.

You can be as original as you dare with your choice, or you can stick to old favourites, such as 'I Believe In Miracles' by Hot Chocolate, with your man doing his best 'Full Monty'. The main thing is to have fun. Remember, though, that the lyrics of a song are important. If a song has the right rhythm but the lyrics are sad, it will be obvious when you watch the tape, and you don't want to end up thinking about the arguments you've had in the past!

Professionally, I have used music in many different ways. Sometimes the result can be really effective, whether you want to create atmosphere or comedy. I use a musician called Strappadictomy, who composes all my music. I was once filming a girl/girl scene in which a trendy young female student was auditioning for a job as a stripper. She seduced the 'suited and booted' model agency manageress, and when her head went down to perform oral sex, I edited in some hip-hop music, which had a sample of an air hostess giving instructions on the plane's emergency exits. The result was as though we were all going down.

Also, remember that music can obscure dialogue, making it a strain to hear what you are saying. This is especially true if the music is nearer to the microphone than you and your partner; if it is just too loud; or if it is very upbeat and pumping while the conversation is slower. Why do you think that the music in adult movies cuts in at the start of the sex? So that you can hear the dialogue at the beginning of the film with the sex supported by a rhythm as well.

Editing and sound

A word of warning. If you are intending to edit the film in any way, you will find that when you make the choices about what shots to put where, in the order that gives you the best result visually, the music will 'jump' about, because you will literally be cutting out big chunks of the soundtrack. The way this is dealt with professionally is to shoot the scene without any music playing at the time, and then edit it in later, as a separate soundtrack. However, this means, for example, that the stripper is dancing to nothing, which is quite difficult, even for an experienced professional. I suggest you have music playing in the background, and that you don't edit the strip part at all, unless you just use half of it in one block.

It's amusing to think when you see a crowd dancing on the set of a film, that they are, in fact, jumping about, smiling and 'getting down' to absolute silence. I think that's why a lot of people on television look as if they can't dance, because it's actually really hard to get 200 people to move in rhythm to nothing.

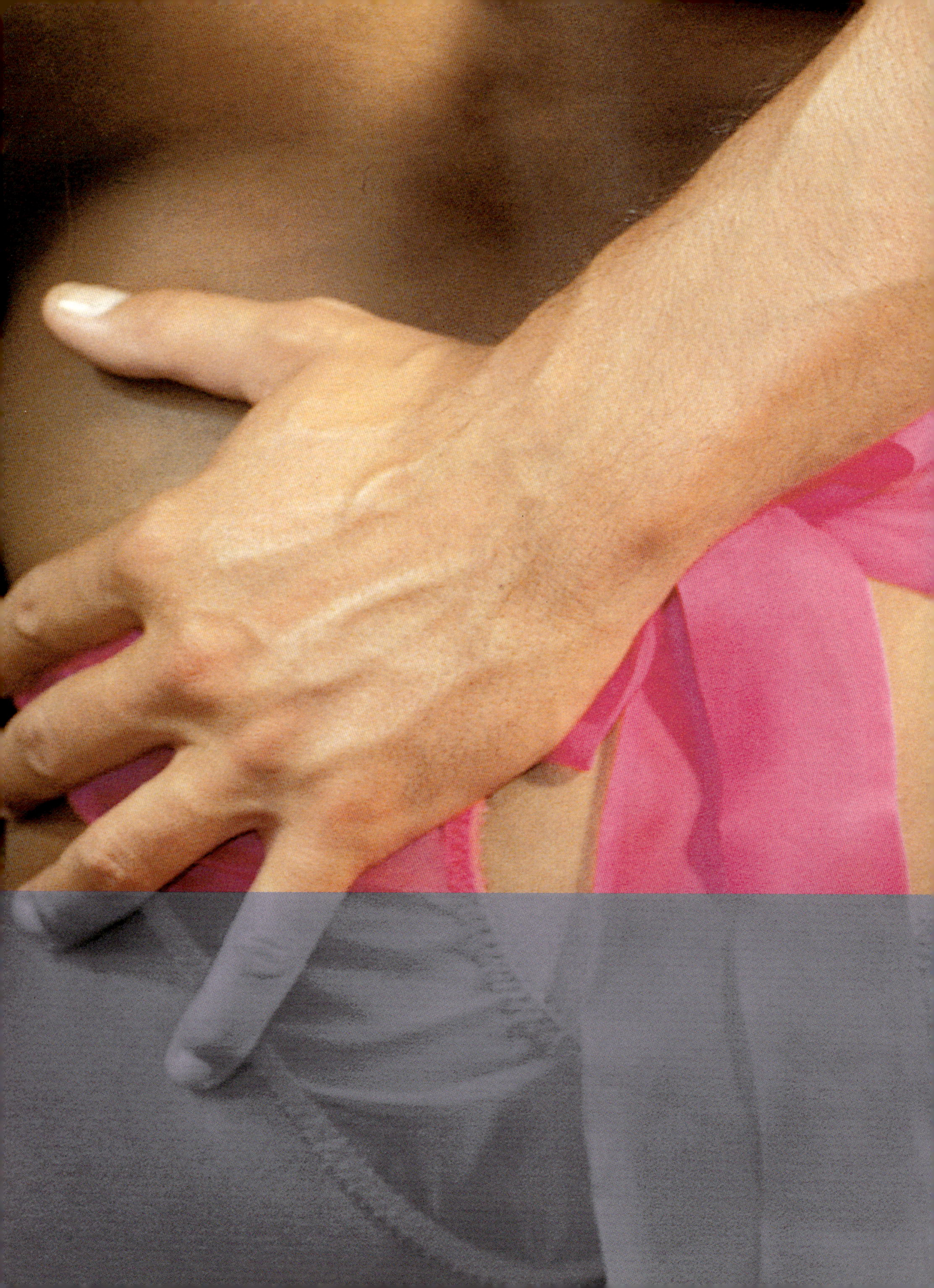

Editing

Your film is in the can – well, almost. All you need to do now, once you've got your breath back, is to go back through all the action and decide exactly which shots you want to keep and which ones don't quite come up to your standards.

At last your sexy body is cast on film in all its glory for your delectation.

Editing

Editing allows you to vary the pace in the movie, letting you build up to the really passionate moments as well as delight in the slower scenes. You can cut away to other scenes and flash backwards or forwards to move a plot along. You can even alter the meaning of the film by how, and who, you edit. My first break making pornographic programmes for commercial release was with Television X, a British-owned adult entertainment satellite channel. For two and half years I not only shot porn at the weekends, but also worked full-time editing porn programmes and films for creative and legal cuts. Editing other people's work showed me how differently various directors approach the job.

THE EDITOR'S CHOICE

During my time at the satellite channel I edited a many of my own films, as well as overseeing various editors working on the edits of my programmes. This also helped me to see how editors approach the same work.

In short, if you have enough of the right footage or 'rushes' – the unedited tape that you have shot – you can edit the same film in a million different ways. They say that there are three films for every film: the writer's film (the way the script appears on paper), the director's film (how it looks on the rushes), and the editor's film (the final product).

The way that you edit your rushes makes all the difference, and can make or break a film. This is why directors often have a strong mistrust of editors! I have even been known to have the occasional argument with editors who have set about my masterpiece with a pair of scissors and some sticky tape.

As I said earlier, the only choices you have available by the time you come to edit are those that you thought about before you started filming and gave yourself while you were directing. The sequences you shot are the only ones at your disposal from which to make a film.

This is an erotic film, so you have a choice. You can make a film that requires little or no editing, just doing it for the experience and to have fun; or you can deliberately film more than you will finally use and give yourself more scope to select and then edit together the best bits.

Good editing conveys mood and excitement.

There is no real need to edit the film if you don't want to. You can just watch the full-length version and fast forward through the boring bits – it's what most people do with edited porn films, anyway. You certainly don't need to buy expensive editing software for your computer. One way to avoid the boring, non-action shots is to use your camera's pause button to stop the action while you are filming, enabling you to change position and then start recording again. You can make the whole film pretty slick using this method, as long as you make sure you record and pause when you intend to.

While we were at college, a group of other students and I made a short film about consumerism. We took over the local sports shop, and asked the assistants to take out boxes and boxes of running shoes for us to film for about two hours. When we returned to view our rushes, all we had were shots of the floor, the bench and the far wall; there were no running shoes! Apparently, when we were filming the shots we wanted, the camera had been on standby, and when we thought we had it on standby, we were, in fact, recording. There is a rather fundamental lesson to be learned here, I think.

Editing software

If you do want to invest in computer equipment to edit your film, there is a wide variety currently on sale. You can start with relatively cheap hardware and software for your home PC, such as the Pinnacle Systems range. But there are also more expensive programmes, such as Adobe Systems' 'Final Cut Pro' or 'Premiere', which you can buy for PC and Apple Mac computers. These produce professional-quality images straight back to your camera via firewire – a high-quality data transfer technology supported by most modern cameras. They cost five or six times more than the cheaper versions, on average, but offer much more advanced functions.

Editing on a computer is much quicker than editing developed film reel, but one problem you may encounter is that digital video takes up huge amounts of memory. You need about 1GB of memory for every five minutes of digital film – so if your unedited film lasts one hour, you will need at least 12GB of memory.

When I edit, I import about 90 minutes of footage on to my computer to make a 20-minute programme or film. Not only will this probably use up all your spare memory, but it may well cause your computer to crash frequently because you are using up most of its resources.

However, if you feel the urge to make a full-blown, edited pornographic epic of many parts, let me point out some of the things you should be thinking about when you start to edit.

Editing 'Gonzo' movies

If you have shot your film in the Gonzo style (see page 101), you will have rushes that basically comprise you following, or bumping into, your partner and talking to them, eventually ending up in bed. The way to edit this is to keep the shots where either you or your partner look or sound good, and then to cut the rest. I always keep any funny lines or particularly good acting, but the basic rule of thumb is to follow the story to its conclusion in the most sexy and entertaining way. Try not to include too many 'dead energy' shots, meaning those that you get bored with when watching or those in which your attention strays. With luck, the result will be a better film.

When I am editing I always watch the 'rough cut' very carefully. That's the edited version with all the elements included but without any the special effects, music, and fine tuning. As I watch, I jot down any mistakes I notice and any improvements that can be made. If I become conscious of my attention wandering, I pause the playback, jot down the time code on the screen (the time individual to each frame), and beside it on my notepad I write 'BORED'. I can then go back and see if the preceding minute is as well edited as I thought, or if I need to make some changes. It may be that the lead-up is a bit slow or the dialogue isn't as 'catchy' as I thought it was. It may simply be that you don't have enough close-ups of the performers and that you feel a little distant from the action as a result.

Editing 'glossy' movies

There are basic rules of narrative editing that you should try to apply if you have shot an introduction to your scene in what you want to appear as the objective style – the glossy studio look.

If you have filmed using the type of shots I defined in the 'Camera Angles' section (see pages 60-61), that is wide, medium and close-up, then the rules are simple (see steps 1, 2 and 3 pictured below).

1 Establish the scene with a wide or long shot, so you will be able to see where, and possibly when, the action is happening.

2 Cut to a medium shot to start to tell the story – you can have several medium shots at this stage as they provide a general viewpoint. Use them until you want to see more action, to move the story on.

3 Cut to a close-up of each person in turn, when they are speaking or carrying out a significant action. You can then cut between the two people with close-up facial or head-and-shoulders shots in an action/reaction sequence. So, if one person says something to which the other person reacts, you cut back and forth between them. It is usual to cut to the person that is speaking at the time, unless you are trying to create a specific effect.

4 When the scene changes or the actors move to another location, the process starts again – from wide through medium to close-up shots.

This sequence is a basic rule of editing still used in most films. You don't have to use this method in order to be able to create something you can enjoy, but it is quite useful to know because it is what you are used to seeing, and what will engage you in the movie. Equally, though, you can do what most pornographers do, and completely ignore the rules of film. I certainly didn't shoot this way for many of my earlier programmes and they still look great.

Filming 'cut-aways'

Imagine you want the two of you in an erotic dance scenario where, for example, the woman is dancing for the man while he sits on the bed and watches. If you film the whole dance from start to finish using a wide shot to encompass the whole action, you will have a problem editing the film. As soon as you cut out any footage, when you play back the edited scene, both of you will suddenly jump from one position to another. This is because you will have removed the footage that showed the transition between the two points, however small that transition was.

A 'cut-away' is a shot from another angle with a different framing, which you would edit in between the two shots where the join is made. A good example of a cut-away in this scenario would be to film a close-up of the man's face to show his reaction to the dance. While you are watching this close-up of the man's face, your mind will unconsciously accept that you are missing part of the dance, which is still happening out of shot.

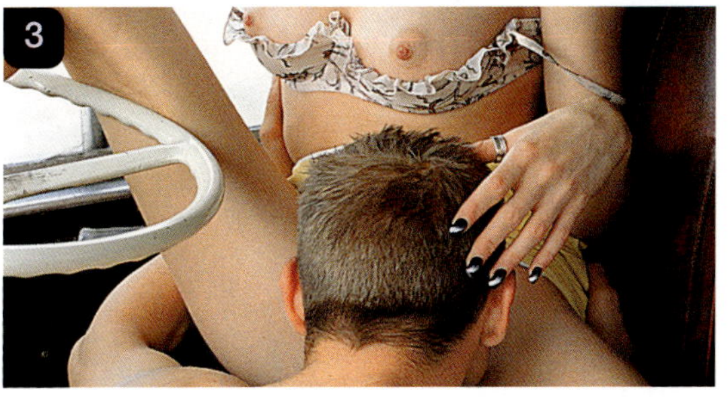

If you think about editing when you are filming, the more options you will have while you edit.

In order to work well, cut-aways need to be placed within a continuous soundtrack. Otherwise, if the sound changes at the same time as the image, your attention will be drawn to the cut and you will realize that the inserted shot is from a different source.

Also, remember only to use cut-aways that are relevant to the scene. One producer, whose films I used to edit while working for TVX used to cut from full-on sex, with three people going at it 'hammer and tongs', to a 'still' of a vase of flowers, and then back to the sex again. It always seemed to me that the sense of reality was somehow lost – wouldn't you agree?

Cut-aways can come in a variety of shapes and sizes, although they are usually close-ups or extreme close-ups as these create more scope for out-of-shot movement and change between two scenes. Examples of good erotic cut-aways include close-ups of hands, lips, eyes or objects which are relevant to the story. The rule to remember is that cut-aways (right) should be filmed at the same time, or as near to the two adjoining shots (above and far right) as possible, so that there is less chance of changes in light, position of props, or the position of your partner. These

differences may seem small when you are filming, in fact, you probably wouldn't even notice them, but they will 'scream' at you once you come to edit your movie.

Continuity

In large professional productions, there a member of staff whose sole responsibility is to keep an eye on the similarities and differences between shots, which would otherwise get missed by a director or performer. You see these people wandering around film sets with instant cameras, taking photos when the crew finish filming a 'take', of the performers' outfits, make-up and furniture.

It isn't just clothes and props that can be a problem. The positions you adopt will probably change from shot to shot. So, remember where you are and how you are positioned at the end of each shot. It is very easy to forget that you have moved your arm up over your head, or your leg over your partner's back. Sometimes you will find that two shots that should, in theory, edit together, just don't and it isn't always obvious why. On closer inspection you see that the continuity has been broken. This is harder to spot when nobody has any clothes on and there are no

grand moves across the room, but they still destroy a smooth edit.

I doubt very much that you will have a continuity person on board for your film, although I'm sure you'd get a lot of offers if you asked around. So it's worth remembering to keep an eye out for any clothes or props changes as you go along – but don't let it ruin the experience. It's quite fun pointing them out in the final film.

Cut-aways help you to link different shots in the same scene more smoothly.

Watching your video

Wow! So now you have your very own adult movie starring you and your porn star partner. At last your sexy body is cast on film in all its glory for your delectation and posterity. So what are you going to do with it?

Well, the most obvious answer is to watch it with your partner. You can both use it to help create a sexy atmosphere and get you in the mood. I highly recommend using porn as a sexual aid with your partner, especially if it's homemade. There is something really hot about watching yourself and your partner having sex while you have sex alongside, in stereo. This is especially

true if both you and your partner have been filmed looking into the camera lens occasionally. The soundtrack alone can be a real turn-on, especially if you don't actually watch the video and just let the sound soak in all over wherever you are playing it.

Why not watch the tape when one of you isn't there? You can use it to stimulate your phone or text sex. One of you can be at home watching the movie, or take it away on a business trip, so that you can both share the experience of one person being able to see the video, and the other not. This is more erotic if the one without is at work, say, or on a train home – where they cannot talk openly in return. You can really get them worked up, willing the journey to end so that they can jump on you in the hallway.

The sequel?

When you've watched the tape enough and you both want to try another one, take a moment to sit back and analyse the first tape. Look at it from every point of view: look at your performance, both on screen and behind the camera. Ask yourself where you could make improvements, where the best shots are, and why, what the lights look like – whether they are flattering, or if there are any heavy shadows. Worse still, can you see any actual lights themselves? Look closely at how your make-up and clothes look under the lights, as they may not have appeared as you had hoped.

If your relationship is open enough you can give constructive criticism and praise to the bits you like or dislike about your partner's performance (tread lightly – none of us are super porn stars).

This is a good time to make note of which angles are most flattering to you. Remember them and make sure you use them next time. If you eliminate as many bad shots as you can each time you make a film, the movies will get better and better.

Your first erotic movie probably won't be your best, but I hope it won't be your last either. The more you get to know your camera and the more you both discover exactly what you like, the better your movies will become. It's all a matter of practice. So turn on the camera, turn on each other, and enjoy yourselves.

I hope you enjoyed the journey through making your own erotic movie and I hope it has given you plenty of ideas to play with. Remember, if at first you don't succeed, enjoy trying it again and again and again! Most of all, I hope you actually give it a go and make your own film. I really like the idea that maybe there are couples everywhere having fun and filming themselves with the help of this book.

If you had a good time and want to find out more about my work, you can visit my website at www.easyote.co.uk and see some of my ideas.

Have fun. Anna xx

Thanks to: Binty Loveridge, Nick Evans, The Shepherd's Pie Club (Abby Tyler, Lisa, Kate and Helen Whiskin, Louise Dear, Lisa Dawson, Claire Wigington), Martin Turnbull, Lisa Gabrielsen, Geilza Silva, Michelle Carter, Henri Brandman, David Lock, Stuart and Val, Helen, Nigel, Allen, all the wonderful models featured, Television X for images, Coco de Mer & Paradiso for underwear and clothes, and my family and friends for their ongoing support. xx

INDEX

Figures in italics indicate captions.

FURTHER READING

Assieter, Alison/Avedon, Carol, *Bad Girls and Dirty Pictures,* Pluto Press 1993

Bachelard, Gaston, *The Poetics of Space,* Beacon Press 1969

Back, Kate & Ken, *Assertiveness at Work,* McGraw-Hill 1992

Bordwell, David & Thompson, Kristin, *Film Art: An Introduction,* McGraw-Hill 1997

Fauer, John, *Shooting Digital Video,* Focal Press 2001.

Friday, Nancy, *Men in Love,* Dell Publishing 1998; *Women on Top,* Pocket Books 1993

Gates, Katharine, *Deviant Desires,* Juno Books 2000

Hill, Philip, *Lacan for Beginners,* Writers & Readers 1997

Kroll, Eric, *Elmer Batters: From the Tip of the Toes to the Top of the Hose,* Taschen 1996

McGillivray, David, *Doing Rude Things,* Sun Tavern Fields 1992

Masoch, Sacher, *Venus in Furs,* Senate 1996

Matrix, Cherie, *Tales from the Clit: A Female Experience of Pornography,* AK Press 1996

Millerson, Gerald, *Video Camera Techniques,* Focal Press 1994

Parker, Tara, *The Book of the Orgasm,* Michael O'Mara Books 1997

Poe, Edgar Allen, *The Philosophy of Composition,* Penguin Books 1986

Ramakas, Micha, *Tom Of Finland,* Benedikt Taschen 2002

Thompson, Bill, *Soft Core,* Cassell Books 1994; *Sadomasochism,* Cassell Books 1994

Williams, Linda, *Hardcore,* Berkeley 1989